Praise for *Broken Walk*

"Gary offers real, raw, and rational discussion on grief after the loss of a child. He brings the practicality of experience and the truth of the Bible to help soothe the parent's suffering soul. Grief is a journey, and Gary leads the reader from hurt to healing."

—Dr. Troy Allen, Pastor,
First Baptist Church College Station

"The grief journey is unique to every grieving parent. Those who are Christians have a God that knows this personally. Jesus, when He walked around among us, experienced grief. He wept. In *Broken Walk: Experiencing God After the Loss of a Child*, Gary Roe uses God's word to create daily readings where the bereaved parent walks with God. The tough questions and emotions are addressed head-on, allowing the reader to experience Jesus, the Balm of Gilead, to make them whole again."

—Glen Lord, Board President,
The Compassionate Friends, President
and CEO, The Grief Toolbox

"Amid the pain and grief from the loss of a child, we look up and ask, "Where is God?" The words "you need to know you are not alone in this" is what separates this book from so many. Pastor and author Gary Roe has once again solidified his status as the go-to resource for people struggling with grief. Keen insight and practical approach are how Gary consistently and compassionately touches on the subjects that grieving parents and grandparents actually need to hear, like "It's ok to grieve". *Broken Walk* takes it to the next level by combining his knowledge as a top grief counselor in with his heart of a Pastor. A must read for parents and families going through the pain of grief."

—Scott Willmore, Senior Pastor,
The Word Community Church

"A bereaved parent's journey is painful, lonely, and overwhelming. *Broken Walk* filters our feelings with faith, reminding us —we are not alone. God walks with us every step of the way."

—Dr. Charles W. Page, MD, author of
A Spoonful of Courage for the Sick and Suffering

"*Broken Walk* is a collection of comforting blankets to wrap around your shoulders when you are feeling the pain of the unthinkable loss of a child. The words speak directly to your grieving heart, reassuring you that you are not alone. The short chapters make it easy to pick up and read for just a few moments at a time."

—Kathy Trim,
Missionary Care and MK Care, TEAM Japan

"Gary Roe is an expert in the field of Grief Recovery. But what is so important now is that Gary now has moved out of the secular grief recovery world and shows us how God can support us and uplift us during our time of loss. Gary Roe weaves through his words and the Scripture he uses, God's Presence and Support that can be used to carry you through this time of loss and separation. Gary describes what a parent who has lost a child is feeling. He then gives the words we need to hear to move forward. I believe it is most important that Gary also explains how to care for yourself through his words and explanations of how God helps you to get through this terrible time in your life. As a Pastor, I would highly recommend this book to any family going through the loss of a child."

—Rev. Louie Lyon, Pastor,
First United Methodist Church,
Sun City

"Gary has done it again! *Broken Walk* hits on all the emotions I have heard bereaved parents speak about during my time as a Chaplain and leading support groups. I believe that all who read this book will be able to relate to the emotions and find comfort, affirmation, and hope. The way faith is incorporated with the grief journey is refreshing. I have not found material that speaks about the challenges of prayer, scripture reading, and church attendance during the grief journey as *Broken Walk* does. I will be using this book for future support groups as I know this is going to help grieving parents break through barriers and into spiritual freedom."

—Jessica D. Wilson,
Hospice Chaplain, Life Coach

"Grief is a daily journey after the loss of a child. Gary Roe has captured the essence of this struggle and provided on-point encouragement for each day of the journey. Well done!"

—Dr. Tony Taylor,
Senior Pastor, Hilltop Lakes Chapel

BROKEN WALK

EXPERIENCING GOD AFTER THE LOSS OF A CHILD

GARY ROE

Broken Walk: Experiencing God After the Loss of a Child
Copyright © 2022 by Gary Roe
All rights reserved.
First Edition: 2022

Print ISBN: 978-1-950382-74-3
KDP Print ISBN: 978-1-950382-73-6
Hardcover ISBN: 978-1-950382-75-0
eBook ISBN: 978-1-950382-72-9

Cover and Formatting: Streetlight Graphics

Published by: Healing Resources Publishing

All Bible references are from THE HOLY BIBLE, NEW INTERNATIONAL VERSION®, NIV® Copyright © 1973, 1978, 1984, 2011 by Biblica, Inc.® Used by permission. All rights reserved worldwide.

The author is not engaged in rendering medical or psychological services, and this book is not intended as a guide to diagnose or treat medical or psychological problems. If you require medical, psychological, or other expert assistance, please seek the services of your own physician or mental health professional.

No part of this book may be reproduced, scanned, or distributed in any printed or electronic form without permission. Please do not participate in or encourage piracy of copyrighted materials in violation of the author's rights. Thank you for respecting the hard work of this author.

Thank you for purchasing *Broken Walk: Experiencing God After the Loss of a Child.*

These pages are designed to be a companion for you in your grief journey.

Please don't read this book just once.

Pick it up again in six months or a year.

Come to it again and again.

Each time you will be at a different place.

You'll see your progress. You'll be encouraged.

And you'll find your hope has grown.

As a thanks, please accept this gift – an exclusive, free, printable PDF for readers of the God and Grief Series.

Download yours today:

Scripture and Prayers from the God and Grief Series

www.garyroe.com/grief-prayers

Other Books by Gary Roe

THE GOD AND GRIEF SERIES:

Grief Walk: Experiencing God After the Loss of a Loved One

Widowed Walk: Experiencing God After the Loss of a Spouse

Orphaned Walk: Experiencing God After the Loss of a Parent (Coming 2022)

THE COMFORT SERIES:

Comfort for Grieving Hearts: Hope and Encouragement in Times of Loss

Comfort for the Grieving Spouse's Heart: Hope and Healing After Losing Your Partner

Comfort for the Grieving Parent's Heart: Hope and Healing After Losing Your Child

Comfort for the Grieving Adult Child's Heart: Hope and Healing After Losing Your Parent

THE GOOD GRIEF SERIES:

Hope in a World Gone Mad: Finding God in Grief, Fear, and Uncertainty

The Grief Guidebook: Common Questions, Compassionate Answers, Practical Suggestions

Grieving the Write Way Journal and Workbook

Aftermath: Picking Up the Pieces After a Suicide

Teen Grief: Caring for the Grieving Teenage Heart

Shattered: Surviving the Loss of a Child

Please Be Patient, I'm Grieving: How to Care for and Support the Grieving Heart

Heartbroken: Healing from the Loss of a Spouse

Surviving the Holidays Without You: Navigating Grief During Special Seasons

THE DIFFERENCE MAKER SERIES:

Difference Maker: Overcoming Adversity and Turning Pain into Purpose, Every Day (Teen Edition; Adult Edition)

Living on the Edge: How to Fight and Win the Battle for Your Mind and Heart (Teen Edition; Adult Edition)

What This Book is All About

"It's okay. You're strong. You'll get through this."

Okay?
Excuse me?
The death of my child is **not** *okay.*
Strong? How can I be strong right now?
Get through this? What is **this***, exactly?*
I'm broken and devastated.

The death of a child is shocking, crushing, heartbreaking, traumatic, and unbelievably painful.

The people around you don't know what to say. They end up saying what they've heard others say.

Perhaps they mean well, but clichés do nothing for a grieving parent or grandparent's heart. Such platitudes only belittle your loss and your pain.

You need something more than this—far more.

You need to know that it's okay to hurt, to be sad, and to grieve.

You need to know that you're not crazy and that your grief is "normal."

You need to know that you're not alone in this.

And most of all, you need the comfort of God's presence.

You need to experience His compassion and love. You need to know He is walking with you in your pain and grief. And that's what *Broken Walk* is all about.

THE DEATH OF A CHILD SHAKES US

The loss of a child breaks our hearts and shakes our souls.

Amid our pain and grief, we look up. We wonder, "Where is God? Did this have to happen? Why?"

Over the last three decades as a missionary, pastor, hospice chaplain, and grief counselor, I've had the honor of walking with thousands of souls through the valley of child loss. Dealing with loss, death, and grief has become my routine.

I now spend my days writing, speaking, and counseling. My focus is simple: meeting grieving hearts – including grieving parents and grandparents—where they are and walking with them there. As we do that together, I believe God speaks, comforts, and brings healing.

God meets us in our pain and embraces us. He walks with us through the emotional pain, mental confusion, physical distress, spiritual questioning, and relational changes.

Jesus journeys with you. As you walk this road, you will feel broken, perhaps even shattered. How could you not?

Jesus personally experienced more pain, suffering, and grief than we can fathom. He knows. He gets it. He is the best grief companion imaginable.

Broken Walk is essentially a grief devotional, designed to be read one chapter a day, though you do not have to read it that way, of course.

Take your time. Open your heart. Be honest about your thoughts and emotions.

Allow Jesus to speak to you in each day's reading.

And remember...

It's okay to hurt.

It's okay to be sad and to grieve.

You are not crazy.

You are not alone.

God is with you in your pain and grief.

God loves you where you are, as you are.

He can bring healing to your broken heart.

He can use this tragedy for great good in your life and in the lives of those you touch.

I'm honored to be with you on this sacred journey.

Breathe deeply.

Take your time.

Read on...

1

How did this happen? How can this be?

My child is gone. How is this even possible?

My heart is stunned, crushed, shattered.

I'm in shock. I feel paralyzed. I stare at the ground in disbelief.

I'm broken. I can't breathe.

What am I going to do?

No, this just can't be. Please, let it not be true.

Lord, help me.

Stunned. Shocked. Immobilized. Crushed. Shattered.

Your heart is broken. It feels like your soul has been torn in two.

Your child is no longer here. How could such a thing happen?

Your mind screams that such things should not happen. This is not the natural order of how things should go. This feels wrong—terribly wrong.

Close your eyes. Take a deep breath.

The Lord is here. He is with you, even in this.

He is here, in this moment. His arms are around you.

Breathe.

Gary Roe

***God is our refuge and strength, an
ever-present help in trouble.
Psalm 46:1***

Lord, I'm stunned, shocked, and shaken. I can barely breathe. Be my strength and my help. You are my refuge.

2

How could this happen?

My heart keeps asking this question—over and over again.

My child cannot be gone. This is simply not possible.

I look for them everywhere – in their room, the living room, kitchen, and bathroom.

I think I hear their voice. My heart leaps. I smile and spin around, expecting to see that familiar face.

It's like a knife being thrust into my soul. I'm shocked, stunned, and crushed all over again.

I'm devastated. My heart is in pieces strewn all over the place. I can barely lift my head.

I don't want to accept this. I can't.

Our hearts are designed to connect. We're created in the image of God. We're wired for relationship.

When your child was born, something miraculous happened. The bond was immediate, unique, deep, and spiritual. In that moment, everything became new.

If you adopted your child, a somewhat different miracle took place. The Lord led you. He prepared your heart and knit it together with theirs. A unique relationship was born.

You're a parent. No wonder you look for your child. Your heart is searching. You want them back. You want them here, now.

Your heart is yearning and longing for them. How could you not? You love them.

Your heart and soul have been struck. The impact is devastating. It feels as though the world has fallen apart—broken beyond repair.

There are no words for it. The loss of your precious child is indescribable.

It's as if all the oxygen has been sucked out of the universe.

The Lord stands with you in this. He knows your pain. He feels it. He knows your heart. He knows you.

---

*"Before you were in your mother's
womb, I knew you."*
Jeremiah 1:5

*Lord, You know me. My heart is crushed.
I can hardly breathe. I need You.*

3

Every morning I wake to a recurring nightmare—a world without my child in it.

The crushing weight of shock and sadness descends upon my chest. The heaviness is suffocating.

I gasp for air. I hyperventilate.

And then the tears start to come.

I shake my head. How can my child be gone?

My day has just begun, and I'm exhausted. My heart feels so tired, so forlorn, so sad.

Sad. I'm so, so sad.

Sad. Such a short word that can express so much.

Sorrowful. Downcast. Dejected. Despondent. Despairing. Melancholy. Mournful. Inconsolable. Broken.

Sad is a powerful word indeed. Yes, this is sad – excruciatingly sad.

Missing your child is hard enough. Knowing that they're not coming back is devastating, gut-wrenching, and even soul-tearing.

The weight on your heart is immense. Sadness is a natural result.

This sadness is healthy because it is real. Your heart is honoring your child. You're expressing your love for them.

The Lord feels your sadness with you. He is with you where you are and accepts you as you are. He is your Father. You are His child. He is closer than you know.

Breathe deeply. Though you may not be able to perceive it, the Lord's love surrounds you. Though He already knows your every thought, share your sadness with Him.

Be merciful to me, Lord, for I am in distress; my eyes grow weak with sorrow, my soul and body with grief.
Psalm 31:9

Father, sorrow grips my heart. Be my comfort. Be my strength.

4

My emotions are so intense.

I feel drained, paralyzed, and confused.

Sometimes all I can do is cry. Other times, I'm so sad that I can't seem to squeeze out a single tear.

Grief surrounds me like a storm cloud. It follows me, wherever I go. The entire world seems dull and lifeless.

I can't think straight. My mind spins and then freezes. My head feels so heavy.

I still can't believe this. How can this be?

I want to hear my child's voice—now.

Grief is a moving target. It never stays still. It's always changing.

Your heart has been broken and crushed. Your grief is intense and runs deep – deeper than you can even yet imagine.

Grieving the loss of a child is an emotional roller-coaster.

There will be steep climbs, sudden curves, and disturbing drops. You'll be jostled and mercilessly thrown about. It will be frustrating, confusing, and even terrifying.

You didn't ask for this. You didn't want it. One terrible day, you found yourself thrust onto this roller-coaster. The safety bar slammed down in front of you, and you found yourself moving in a direction you didn't want to go.

Though the world looks the same, everything has changed. Loss has invaded and grief has taken over. The emotional storm cloud is your constant companion.

Thankfully, you have another companion—the Lord Jesus Christ. He is in your grief cloud with you.

He knows grief and pain well. He is with you each and every moment.

Your grief honors your child. Your heart is expressing your love for them. Share your heart with Jesus. Pour out your grief to Him.

God created you to love. You're expressing the heart He gave you.

***Be strong and take heart, all you
who hope in the Lord.
Psalm 31:24***

*Father, this grief is confusing. My feelings are so
intense. Strengthen me. Give me hope.*

5

Is this my fault?

Did I fail?

I didn't protect them. Surely, I could have done something to prevent this.

I'm the parent. Protection is my job.

I protected them since they were born. I swore that I would take care of them and never let anything harm them.

When bad things happened, I blamed myself.

Now, my child is gone, and my thoughts torture me day and night.

I'm a terrible parent.

What parent can't protect their own child?

God blesses us with children. He Himself forms them in the womb. Each one is planned, wanted, and personally created by Him.

We were witnesses and participants in the miraculous birth process—from conception until our child's first breath. We were stunned and awestruck.

Love wells up within and begins to pour out of us onto this miraculous new life in our arms. We intuitively sense their complete vulnerability. They are totally dependent on us.

Part of love is provision and protection. It's our job to provide what they need and protect them from harm. This God-given instinct is strong in us as parents. Our sense of responsibility is huge and heavy.

No matter how old our kids are, those original parental instincts remain. All it takes is a need or a danger to activate them.

Now they're gone, as if they were ripped from our watchful arms. We blame ourselves. We didn't protect them.

Logically, you know that you're not all-powerful or all-knowing. Yet as a parent, you expect yourself to be both.

No wonder you're devastated. The emotional pain is more than words can possibly describe.

Share with the Lord what's happening inside you. Tell Him about this powerful sense of guilt and responsibility within you. He understands. He is the ultimate Parent.

Find healthy ways to express this festering guilt. Get it out. Release it to the Lord.

You have searched me, Lord, and you know me.
You know when I sit and when I rise;
you perceive my thoughts from afar.
Psalm 139:1-2

Lord, the guilt eats me alive some days. I release this crushing weight to You. Lift it from me. For the mistakes I made, I receive Your complete and total forgiveness through your Son.

6

I miss my child.

My heart is like liquid and leaking out all over everything.

I try to be strong. When the grief comes, I try to fight it off, put a good face on it, and be as normal as possible.

But things aren't normal. Nothing is normal. Everything has changed.

My world feels so empty.

I'm a mess. I can't seem to hold anything inside for long.

I feel sick inside, like some deep part of me is broken and beyond repair.

I miss my child, and the missing is so intense.

Like a wounded animal, I want to withdraw and hide.

Life has changed. The world suddenly feels empty, cold, unkind, and even dangerous.

You're created in the image of God. You're unique in human history. There has never been another person exactly like you, and there never will be again.

The same is true of your child.

Unique. Special. Valuable beyond description. Priceless.

From even before you saw them, your hearts were connected.

They were a separate little person, but they were a part of you—and you were a part of them.

This is true even now. You are still connected, even though they are gone from your sight.

Your heart has been torn. Grief is leaking out everywhere. This is natural and healthy. Unfortunately, the world isn't friendly to grieving hearts. It can be cold and unfeeling.

The Lord knows grief well. He knows you. He loves you and is walking with you in this mess. You are special to Him. He knows and feels your pain.

Cling to Him. You are already in His embrace. Open your heart to Him. Hide nothing.

I lift up my eyes to the mountains—where does my help come from? My help comes from the Lord, the Maker of heaven and earth.
Psalm 121:1-2

*Lord, I feel broken. My heart is shattered.
Speak to me. My help comes from You.*

7

*It was all so sudden. My child was here
one moment and gone the next.*

*How does that happen? Why? What am I
supposed to do now? What's next?*

I can't wrap my mind around this terrible reality. My heart can't grasp it. I know it's true, but I can't seem to accept it.

*I don't know what to do. I'm caught between
two worlds: what was and what is.*

Please, can't things just go back to the way they were?

I want my child back. I feel empty and lifeless without them.

Death seems sudden even if it's anticipated. Life always departs in an instant.

This is especially true when we lose a child.

Your love for your child is so clear and evident. Of course, your heart can't process this, at least not fully. Your mind is trying to make sense of this somehow.

It's difficult to understand something you don't want to be true. Your heart naturally doesn't want to accept this awful separation.

You're designed by God to love and be loved. Your heart was

drawn to your child, perhaps even before they were in the womb. When your heart attaches, it clings. Love endures.

You feel this tension. You love your child, but they're not here anymore. How can this be?

God walks with you in this strange new place. Trust Him with your shattered heart. Pour out your thoughts and feelings to Him. He knows all about the path you are walking.

He loves you. All that you need today is in Him.

"The Lord himself goes before you and will be with you; He will never leave you nor forsake you. Do not be afraid; do not be discouraged."
Deuteronomy 31:8

Lord, I don't know how to do this. I give You my shattered heart. I have no words. I cry out to You.

8

Lord, I don't know how to think about this. You are with me. You never leave. Help me. Guard my heart.

Children are everywhere. I see other families everywhere I go—even on my computer and TV screen.

Parents and children are together everywhere, smiling and laughing.

My heart breaks—again. It shatters into more and more pieces. Soon there will be nothing left of it.

The pain is indescribable. There are no words for it.

I feel so sad, devastated, and angry. I'm beginning to resent the happiness I see in others.

Sometimes I can't get enough air. I feel like I'm suffocating.

I want to hide.

What has happened to me? Who am I becoming?

I know what has happened. My child has died. They are no longer here, and the black hole in my soul seems to be expanding.

The pain is beyond words.

Seeing other parents with their children becomes painful and even shocking. Every visual of a child or family slices our hearts, and grief comes spewing out.

Stunned. Sad. Irritated. Confused. Angry. As bereaved parents, we feel all of this and much more. We see another child and our souls writhe with pain and longing.

How could this happen? Why our child? Why now? Why this way? Why?

This is wrong. Unfair. Backwards. Wrong. Such things should not happen.

No other loss we have endured or could ever face compares. In a world packed full of other children, parents, and families, just walking outside can feel emotionally dangerous.

The intensity of our mourning shouts how unique and special our child was and is.

God is with you in this deep, dark valley. He surrounds you. He is the ultimate Father. He knows and feels your pain.

Though you might not feel it, His love for you is perfect. His arms are around you. He speaks to you continually, even though it seems like you can hear nothing.

Release the grief within. As much as possible, express it as it comes. You are not alone.

If I say, "Surely the darkness will hide me
and the light become night around me,"
even the darkness will not be dark to you;
the night will shine like the day,
for darkness is as light to you.
Psalm 139:11-12

Lord, guard my heart. Protect me from bitterness.
You know my thoughts. I give my heart and life
to you. Help me, empower me, to be
real and honest with You.

9

I feel nervous. I seem to be anxious all the time.

Sometimes, I find myself holding my breath. Other times, I can't get enough air.

It's like I'm hyperventilating almost all the time.

My child is no longer here. I feel vulnerable—like everyone I love and care about is in danger.

I tremble. I can't think straight. My mind wanders. My emotions are all over the place.

I wake up anxious. I walk around anxious. I go through the day anxious. I go to bed at night anxious.

It's like I've been hijacked. Anxiety has invaded and taken me hostage.

Your world has changed. Someone you love deeply – your precious child—is no longer here. Everything is different now.

Your mind is attempting to understand this. Your heart is shattered. Emotion is spilling out everywhere. Many things seem uncertain—perhaps everything. Anxiety is a natural result.

No one enjoys being anxious. We want to understand. We want peace of mind and heart.

The Lord is with you in this anxiety-ridden, unknown territory you find yourself in. His arms are around you. He invites you to breathe and to be patient with yourself.

You're in uncharted territory. That can be unnerving and anxiety-producing. Be kind to yourself. Rest in the Lord's embrace. Share your anxiety with Him. Surrender your fears, one by one. Talk to Him. Keep talking.

Breathe. See yourself in Jesus' arms. Know that He lives in you. You are in Him.

Search me, God, and know my heart;
test me and know my anxious thoughts.
See if there is any offensive way in me
and lead me in the way everlasting.
Psalm 139:23-24

Father, You know my anxious thoughts. You are
with me. In my anxiety, I look to You.

10

The anxiety is getting worse. Sometimes it takes over.

My heart rate jumps. I nearly pass out. I can't catch my breath.

When it strikes, I'm terrified. Am I having panic attacks?

It's awful. Fear is growing inside me. I feel out of control. My emotions and body betray me.

On top of this, these episodes are embarrassing. I fall apart in public. I find myself afraid of going certain places or even of going out at all.

What's happening to me? Is something wrong? Am I going crazy?

I want my child back. I want things to be the way they were. Please.

Anxiety and panic attacks are common in grief – and very common after the loss of a child.

This profound, deep loss naturally raises our anxiety baseline. We feel more nervous, less focused, and more vulnerable.

All this can be frightening. We don't feel like ourselves. We often feel overwhelmed and out of control. It's completely natural to wonder if we're losing it. Anxiety and wondering about our sanity are part of the grief process.

When the panic comes, breathe. Tell yourself, "This will pass."

You're not going crazy but losing your child has thrust you into what feels like an insane situation.

Acknowledge the anxiety and panic. Be honest with the Lord about your fears and anxieties. List them, and then lay them before the Lord, one by one. Release, and then keep releasing.

The Lord is with you. Rest in Him. Share with Him. Be honest and real. He loves you.

I waited patiently for the Lord; He turned to me and heard my cry. He lifted me out of the slimy pit, out of the mud and mire; He set my feet on a rock and gave me a firm place to stand.
Psalm 40:1-2

Lord, I feel like a mess. You are with me in this. Calm my heart. I trust You are guiding me through this.

11

No one should have to bury their children.

That's an old saying, and it's so true. This is backwards. It's all wrong somehow.

Parents have children. Parents raise children. Parents release their kids into the world.

Parents keep being parents, until the parents die. The baton gets passed. The kids live on. This is the natural order of things.

Parents should die first. My child should be here. I should be gone.

My heart is having trouble accepting this nightmare. I don't want to accept it. I want my child back. I want things the way they used to be.

No parent should ever have to experience this.

Wrong. It's all wrong.

Yes, this feels wrong and out of order.

People are born, live their lives, and then pass on. Grandparents pass on first, then parents, and then the children, and so on. We see this as the natural order of life.

When the expected order is upended, we're stunned and shaken. We blink, shake our heads, and crumble inside. Everything feels wrong.

Our connection with our children is powerful and deeply spiritual. In most cases, their death is not something we expect, prepare for, or even care to contemplate.

We know that the natural order of things gets upended frequently. We know that life is unpredictable and does not work according to our plans and desires. Yet this still seems wrong. Very wrong.

Share your pain, confusion, and frustration with the Lord. Release your thoughts and emotions to Him. Ask Him to provide safe people you can vent to and talk freely with.

The Lord is close to the brokenhearted. He is closer than you know.

He heals the brokenhearted and
binds up their wounds.
Psalm 147:3

Lord, this terrible loss feels backwards and out of place.
I choose to walk with You in all this. Comfort
and restore my broken heart.

12

I'm scared. I'm afraid of what might happen next.

If this can happen, what else might?

It's dawning on me that almost anything can happen to anyone at any time. This includes me and everyone I love and care about.

That's terrifying. Suddenly, the world seems a very unsafe and dangerous place.

My child is gone. I wonder, "Who's next?"

I want to protect myself and those I love, but I don't know how. Perhaps I can't. After all, I couldn't protect my own child.

I'm stunned at how little I can control. I feel helpless and scared.

Fear can be a huge part of grief. When a child dies, all kinds of hidden terrors get triggered. Our world gets turned upside down. Life seems less safe and more threatening.

Fear comes knocking on the door of our hearts. When it does, we tend to do better when we acknowledge it and then feel our way through it. Trying to not be afraid only causes our minds to dwell more on the fear.

Express your fears to God. Share with Him what you're afraid of. He knows already. He loves you and longs for you to talk with Him about what's happening inside you.

Acknowledge the fear and get it out. Don't let these terrors go underground and rule your heart. Writing, talking, drawing, and even exercising can all be done in a spirit of prayer.

Share with God what you're feeling. Keep being honest and real with yourself and with Him.

You are my hiding place; you will protect me from trouble and surround me with songs of deliverance.
Psalm 32:7

Lord, You know my fears. You are my hiding place.
You protect me in ways I'm not aware of.

13

My mind is constantly spinning.

I can't settle. I can't rest. I'm having trouble sleeping.

I think of my child constantly. I think about us, our family, and the way life used to be.

I miss my child so desperately. Everything has changed.

If I'm engaged in something or out with people, I seem to do better. As soon as I'm alone, however, my brain goes bonkers.

My thoughts and feelings are all over the place. I'm on a mental merry-go-round, and I can't get off.

Restless. Unsettled. Anxious. Nervous. Scared.

I don't like this at all.

When our child dies, our personal worlds are forcefully altered. We're stunned. We try to figure out what happened and why. We wonder what will happen next, what we should be doing, and how all this is going to work out.

Our brains are in upheaval. Our minds spin—around and around. This is natural and common for grieving parents.

Try slowing those thoughts down by writing or drawing. Get what you're thinking down on paper, no matter how ridiculous some of it might seem. Express it. Get it out.

God is with you, listening and guiding. Try writing to Him, openly and honestly. The more you do this, the more manageable this mental treadmill will likely become.

The loss of your child hits your entire being, including your mind. It can feel like the universe itself is shaking. Be kind to yourself. This is excruciatingly hard.

Yes, my soul, find rest in God; my
hope comes from Him.
Psalm 62:5

Father, bring peace to my mind. Cause me
to rest in You. You are my peace.

14

*I woke up in the middle of the night. I
thought I heard my child calling me.*

*Perhaps I was dreaming, but it seemed so real. The truth is
that I've heard that call many times since their death.*

*At first, my heart leaps. One time, I even answered.
Then the reality comes crashing in.*

They're gone.

*I wonder how many times they called me, and I didn't hear?
And how many times they needed me, and I wasn't there?*

Were they thinking of or calling for me at the end?

This is torture. Pure torture.

*I can almost hear them calling me now. Perhaps my
longing to hear their voice causes this. I don't know.*

Our child's voice is one of a kind. We've heard it so many times that their voice has taken up residence in our hearts. It echoes inside us. Deep down, we hear them calling.

We love our kids. We meet their needs. When a child dies, we naturally wonder if we did everything we could have along the way. What did we miss? Was there a need we didn't meet? Did they ever call for us, and we didn't hear or respond?

This incessant internal questioning can be torturous indeed.

The parent-child bond is deep. There's no other relationship like it.

Bereaved parents need to talk. We need to say our child's name and share our memories. We need to air our questions, frustrations, and confusion. Grieving parents need to express what's happening inside.

We need to cry out to our Father. He is here. He hears every cry.

He invites us to trust Him enough to unload and release. He knows what we're feeling and experiencing, and He waits for us to share freely and honestly with Him.

Resist the tendency to isolate and hide. In times of great pain, we tend to distance ourselves. Ask for grace and ability from Him to stay open and receptive.

Lord, we need you so desperately, all the time, every day. We need to hear your voice today. Hear the cry of our hearts.

---

*Evening, morning and noon I cry out
in distress, and he hears my voice.*
Psalm 55:17

*Lord, guard me from pulling away from You or from
those You want to walk with me through all this. Keep
my broken heart open. I need Your healing.*

15

I feel rejected.

My friends have changed, especially those who are parents.

They're avoiding me. They don't call, text, or email anymore. They don't invite me out.

I don't fit in anymore. I've lost a child.

When I see other children and families, grief surges up within me. My child is gone. What am I supposed to do?

These people used to be my friends. Now, it's like I have some contagious disease.

I'm mad, frustrated, confused, and hurt. I feel like everything I had has been taken from me, and I keep losing more along the way.

Isn't losing my child more than enough? Do I have to lose my friends too?

We have relationships with other parents and families. When we lose a child, our entire relational network is upended. This is natural, and even inevitable. But it's also frustrating, confusing, and painful.

You've been thrust into a new world that looks the same but where all the rules are different. The loss of a child is terrifying to a parent. When other parents see you, most don't know what to do or say. They think about their own children and shudder. They unconsciously and silently distance themselves. They become shadow friends and reminders of the power of this terrible loss.

You might feel abandoned, rejected, and even betrayed. The pain can strike deep and begin to plant seeds of bitterness inside you.

The Lord knows all about being an outcast. He continually experiences rejection. He's also an expert at forgiveness.

Jesus, the Forgiving Outcast, lives in you. He understands. He loves you.

He can also empower you to forgive so that your heart is not repeatedly crushed by what others might say or do. He knows. He gets it. Cry out to Him.

"So do not fear, for I am with you; do not be dismayed, for I am your God. I will strengthen you and help you; I will uphold you with my righteous right hand." Isaiah 41:10

*Lord, You live in me. You will never leave me or abandon me.
Fill me and empower me to forgive.*

16

My mind is foggy. I can hardly think.

I forget things. My head feels heavy.

I go out into the world, but it's like I'm not there. Everything looks the same, but everything feels different.

My child is gone, and I don't know what to do.

I'm exhausted. My sleep pattern is off. I can't stop thinking about them and their death.

Memories assault me. They are like thorns in my soul.

I want my old life back. I don't like this new one. It's painful, confusing, exhausting, and desperately lonely.

Mental fog and fatigue are common in grief. Our child has departed, and life is not the same. Our lives and hearts are forever different.

This is all too much for our brains. We shift into maintenance mode. Again, it's like being hit by a truck. We're stunned and immobilized.

While we recover, our minds are foggy. Our thinking is less sharp. The loss of a child packs a cognitive wallop.

Don't expect yourself to cruise through this unaffected. Your thinking, concentration, work performance, and energy will naturally be impacted.

You are not yourself right now. Life is not the same. You are not the same.

You don't have to be on the top of your game to experience God, heal, recover, and grow. Accept yourself where you are, as you are. God does. He is kind to you. Be kind to yourself.

***Restore to me the joy of Your salvation
and grant me a willing spirit,
to sustain me.
Psalm 51:12***

*Lord, I'm exhausted. I feel like a shadow of my
former self. Support me. Sustain me.*

17

Food doesn't taste the same. Frankly, I don't want to eat.

Sometimes I end up skipping meals because I simply forget to eat. I'm not hungry. I have no appetite.

When I do eat, nothing tastes good. Every meal reminds me my child is no longer here.

Nothing seems to feel good either. Perhaps I'm growing numb.

What's happening to me?

Life as I knew it has disappeared. Maybe I disappeared along with it.

The loss of a child pounds our entire system. The resulting grief strikes our taste buds too. We find ourselves eating mechanically – not for pleasure, but for survival.

Some have no appetite and eat less and less. Others eat more and more. Our grief tends to drive us one way or the other.

When death strikes our child, parts of us seem to die too.

Find ways to express the changes you're experiencing. Talk. Write. Pray. This is part of "getting the grief out."

When you're honest with God and yourself about what's happening to you and inside you, you honor your child. Expressing your grief and pain is one way you can still say, "I love you."

As you process your grief in healthy ways, your appetite will eventually return. Over time, things will most likely even out again, but they will not be the same as before. Life has changed now. Your world has been altered.

Tell the Lord about this. Share your heart with Him. Even if you don't feel His presence, He's there. He is your water amid this desert of grief.

As the deer pants for streams of water,
so my soul pants for you, my God.
Psalm 42:1

Lord, remind me that now is not forever. Though I feel stuck, I trust that You are at work.

18

*Losing my child is impacting all my
relationships, especially my marriage.*

*We're both parents, but we're dealing with this so differently.
I had hoped that perhaps this would bring us closer
together. We need each other now more than ever.*

*Instead of bringing us together, this intense
grief seems to be driving us apart.*

*Neither one of us knows what to do. When one of
us wants to talk, the other doesn't. When one of us
wants to try this or that, the other doesn't.*

*It's like some insidious sort of creeping separateness
invaded our family. Like a huge grenade went
off and blew us all in different directions.*

*No one knows what to do. And we tend
to take it out on each other.*

We must find a way to come together. We must.

*I feel smacked from every angle. Everything
seems to be falling apart.*

When a child dies, our family changes forever. If we're married, our marriage changes too.

To say that we're different is a gross understatement. In marriage, two one-of-a-kind, unique individuals become one. We each had a unique relationship with the child we lost. We think, feel, and process things differently, yet together.

Both parents have lost a son or daughter. The marriage will never be the same.

None of our relationships will stay the same. This loss changes everything because it changes us.

Amid the pain and grief of the loss of our child, the shaking of our marriage can be overwhelming and frightening. We can feel like our entire life is slipping away from us.

Jesus has the amazing ability to meet us where we are, as we are. Even as we grieve, He wants to work in and through us to meet our mate and partner where they are, as they are. Jesus can empower us to do this for them, even if they can't seem to do the same for us.

"Accept one another, just as God in Christ has accepted you" (Romans 15:7), the Apostle Paul tells us. Accepting our spouse where they are at present is a huge step toward greater understanding and love.

This is hard. So many different things come into play. We need wisdom, patience, comfort, reassurance, and a whole lot of love. All these things are in Jesus.

Ask Him for what you need. Try not to hold back. Ask. Seek. Knock.

"Ask and it will be given to you; seek and you will find; knock and the door will be opened to you."
Matthew 7:7

Broken Walk

Lord, I feel like I have nothing left. My tank is empty. Fill me with Yourself. Be my fuel for this journey. Work in me and love my mate through me. Bring us together.

19

Someone asked me yesterday what I miss the most. I was glad they asked, but I was stunned for a moment. I didn't know how to answer.

I found myself saying, "I miss my child's presence—just them being here." Then, of course, I lost it. Emotion surged up and out. The tears flowed like a river.

A person's presence is more powerful than I could have imagined.

No matter where I look, my child is not there. Only in pictures, videos, and in my heart.

Their presence is gone. My life and world feel so empty.

I limp through the day, going through the motions. My child's absence permeates everything.

It feels like my heart has disappeared, and I'm just going through the motions.

A person's presence is powerful indeed. When we're with someone we love, our hearts respond. We feel safe. We drop our guard a bit. We become real and authentic. Life is about loving and being loved.

When a child departs, the hole they leave is massive. It seems to encompass everything. We become hyperaware of their absence. We can't see them or be with them. Our hearts long for them. We mourn.

Without our child, the whole world can seem empty and meaningless.

God wired your heart for relationship. Your bond with your child is deep, powerful, and unique. No wonder this hurts to the core of your being.

Don't let this pain fester inside. Keep being real with your heavenly Father about what's happening inside you. Get in the habit of sharing everything with Him. Tell him what you miss.

Lean into Him. Let Him carry you. Grieving well is not about being strong or trying harder. It's about trusting God, even when nothing seems to make sense.

Then Job replied: "If only my anguish could be weighed, and all my misery be placed on the scales! It would surely outweigh the sand of the seas— no wonder my words have been impetuous."
Job 6:2-3

Father, I miss my child so much. Even though the loss hurts, thank You for the love between us. Thank You for placing them in my life.

20

I've thought more about what I miss.

It's not just my child's presence. It's everything.

I miss everything about them. I miss their voice, their smile, and their laughter. I miss their touch.

I miss all that we had. I miss the quirks that frustrated me so much. I miss our family.

I miss my child. I miss everything about them.

My heart is broken and aching. The pain is excruciating.

I don't know how to do this.

When a child dies, we lose not only them but also much that was attached to them.

These losses hit us, again and again, over time. It can seem like we discover new losses almost every day.

Some days, it can feel like we've lost everything. The grief is heavy, even crushing.

I think of Job in the Old Testament. He experienced multiple, heavy losses, all on top of each other. He endured the loss of all his children in a single day. Sudden. Traumatic. Devastating.

Job's losses would have killed most of us. He felt the pain. He was emotionally overwhelmed and physically debilitated. He had questions—lots of them.

In the midst of it all, he did what he knew to do.

He expressed his grief. He kept presenting his broken, shattered heart to the One who created him.

He clung to God.

> *My eyes have grown dim with grief; my whole frame is but a shadow. Job 17:7*

Lord, cause me to be honest and open with You. You know it all already, and You love me.

21

Work is a challenge now, and that's an understatement. Some days it's impossible.

I'm going through the motions. I'm only half there at best.

Sometimes I don't think I'm there at all.

I can't think straight. My mind wanders. My thoughts keep coming back to my child.

I'm in a fog most of the day. Work distracts me from my grief, and yet grief permeates my work at the same time.

I wear my loss wherever I go. My coworkers are watching. I can feel it.

Just getting out of bed is a chore. Work feels like a massive, unclimbable mountain.

No matter where I am, I feel alone.

The loss of a child affects every part of life. Our souls shake. Drastic, traumatic change has occurred, and now it is trickling down to every part of our existence.

Work is, of course, a huge challenge. Life is not business as usual. Your heart, mind, soul, and body are all powerfully impacted by this terrible, unthinkable loss. Your work will be too.

Yes, other people are watching. That's okay. You can't change that. You can only take care of you.

Focus on taking your heart seriously. Invest your time and energy in grieving in healthy ways.

Good self-care is not selfish. Taking care of yourself is one way to honor God and your child, and to love those around you. In fact, a healthy you is one of the best gifts you can give to others.

The Lord will guide and teach you. He's providing for you each and every moment. Good self-care begins with resting in Him.

Trust in the Lord with all your heart. Don't lean on your own understanding. In all your ways acknowledge Him, and He will direct your paths.
Proverbs 3:5-6

Father, guide and empower me at work. Live through me in this grief wilderness. Keep my eyes on You.

22

I think I'm losing it. I keep thinking I see my child.

Walking across the street. In a crowd at a restaurant. Next to me in the car. At church. In the grocery store.

It doesn't seem to matter where I am or what I'm doing.

It's like my child is now the lens through which I see the world. I know they're not here, yet they're everywhere.

Their absence follows me. Wherever I am, they're not there. They're absent here, there, and everywhere.

This is too much for my shattered heart.

What in the world do I do with this?

Our hearts seem to have eyes, don't they?

We often see what we want to see. We sometimes see what our hearts are longing for.

The loss of a child, no matter what age, is traumatic and terribly painful. Our hearts and minds can't handle the onslaught of all that this means. We must take it in increments—one day, one little bit at a time.

We swear we can still hear their voice. We seem to see them here and there. We're continually aware of their absence. It feels like our hearts break again and again.

Memories come. Emotions rise. Thoughts invade, swirl around, and depart again. This is draining and exhausting.

God is our strength. In fact, we have no true strength outside of Him. He gives us life and holds us together.

When we're standing, He holds us up. When we're sitting, He holds us. As we grieve, He holds us. As we question Him, He holds us.

He holds us because He loves us.

He loves you. He holds you. All the time. Everywhere. No matter what.

He will never leave you or forsake you—no matter how things might look or feel. He will never let you go.

I love you, Lord, my strength. The Lord is
my rock, my fortress and my deliverer;
my God is my rock, in whom I take refuge, my shield
and the horn of my salvation, my stronghold.
Psalm 18:1-2

Lord, this all feels so traumatic. You are my life and
my strength. Remind me that You love me and hold
me. Remind me that You will never let me go.

23

Where did everyone go?

First, my child died. Then everyone else began disappearing.

Many said they would be here for me. Where are they?

Lots of promises of support, but no follow through. No calls, texts, emails. Nothing.

Is there something wrong with me?

I've never asked much of anything from others. Now, when I need them, they're nowhere to be found.

My child's death was more than enough. I hadn't expected this too.

If it helps any, what you're experiencing is all too common. Grieving parents often feel isolated and even rejected.

At first, you get inundated with condolences and attention, and then poof—nothing.

Most people will give you about a month to grieve, and then they'll expect you to be back to your normal self. The problem is that you're not who you were. You're different now. Your world has changed. This deep loss has changed you.

People don't know what to do with your grief. No wonder you feel lonely.

God understands. He is the most misunderstood, ignored, and

rejected being in the universe. He knows all about this kind of relational pain.

He shares your loneliness with you. He knows your confusion, frustration, and pain. His love for you is beyond measure. Lean into Him. Rest again in His embrace.

And so we know and rely on the love God has for us. God is love.
1 John 4:16

When I feel alone, Lord, let me remember You. I will rely on Your love for me.

24

I'm angry with God.

I've been hiding this. I've been scared to admit it. I know I shouldn't be angry with Him, but I am.

After all, He could have done something. He could have stopped this. He could have saved my child. He could have healed them.

Instead, He let them die. I feel like He took them away—from me and everyone else who loved them.

I don't understand. I don't get it. It doesn't make sense.

I'll never understand. All the clichés I hear mean nothing.

God, why?

Questioning God in times of loss is natural, and especially so when a child dies. This death seems so wrong, out-of-order, and backwards.

Most bereaved parents get angry with God at some point in their grief journey. We want our child back. It doesn't matter how old they were.

We're angry. Anger looks for a target. We look for someone to blame. For most of us, the buck stops with God.

God is well acquainted with anger. He knows our hearts and minds. He knows our distress and frustration. He is not surprised by anything we think or feel.

Since God already knows when you're angry, try expressing your anger to Him. Be honest. Be real. Don't hold back.

God knows your heart. He can handle it. Pray it out. Write it out. Talk out loud to Him.

Begin to make it a habit to express what you're thinking and feeling to Him without reservation. Share your heart as fully and as completely as possible.

God wants and longs for you to share your heart with Him. He loves you.

My eyes are dim with grief. I call to you, Lord, every day; I spread out my hands to you.
Psalm 88:9

God, I'm angry. I have questions. You know my heart. Help me to be real with You.

25

I can't believe what people will say.

If I hear, "At least they're in a better place," or "At least you had them this long," or at least anything one more time, I'm going to scream.

"God needed another angel." Really? Why in the world would someone say that?

People don't see me, do they? What are they thinking? Don't they know how bad I'm hurting?

People just don't get it. They don't understand. Maybe they can't.

First, they disappear. Then, when I do see them, they utter niceties and platitudes.

Not helpful. Not helpful at all.

My child is gone. There are no words for this.

You're right. People don't understand. Unless they've been there themselves, the best they can do is sympathize.

They feel uncomfortable. They don't know what to say, so they end up saying what they've heard others say.

Perhaps they're terrified of losing their own child. Your loss unearths their greatest fear.

People don't like pain. When they suddenly find themselves in the presence of suffering, they don't know what to do. It would be nice if they simply stayed silent, but few manage to do this.

What people say is far more about them than it is about you or your child. Out of the mouth, the heart speaks.

Try not to make their words about you. What they say and do is about them and what's going on in their minds and hearts.

God is the ultimate listener. He's perfect at it. He's listening to your heart now.

He feels your pain and frustration. You won't get clichés and platitudes from Him. You'll get His constant presence and His eternal love.

"I have heard many things like these; you are miserable comforters, all of you!"
Job 16:2

People don't understand, but You do. Lord, You know me. You love me. Comfort me today.

26

I feel confused.

I know what happened. I know I miss my child terribly. I know I feel alone in my grief.

I don't know what life looks like now. I don't know what's ahead.

I keep trying to figure things out, but my mind ends up going in circles. I'm stuck on a treadmill, and I can't step off.

I don't know what to do. I don't know how to feel. I don't know what to say.

Everything has changed. It feels like I'm in a free fall with no safety net.

I hang my head a lot. I sigh continually. I want this to be over, but I have no idea what that means.

I want my child back, but I know that's not going to happen.

I'm broken and confused.

Loss this deep brings so much change with it. The death of a child changes everything.

The ripple effects are pervasive and stunning. Nothing in our lives is left untouched.

Our minds try to make sense of it. Our hearts are wired for

connection. The parent-child bond is extraordinary and permanent. Separation like this doesn't compute.

You're in uncharted territory. You've had other losses, but this loss is completely different.

You've never been here before—and you never wanted to be. The landscape—this trackless wasteland of child-loss-grief—is foreign and foreboding.

You don't know what's coming next.

Confusion is natural and common. Nothing seems to make sense anymore.

The Lord knows. He knows your pain and confusion. He knows the path ahead.

Lean into Him and let Him lead, one step at a time.

But now, Lord, what do I look
for? My hope is in you.
Psalm 39:7

Lord, You know my confusion. I will express my
thoughts, worries, and fears to You. Empower me to
be honest and real. You are my hope and safety.

27

I wonder about a lot of things these days.

Where exactly is my child now? What are they doing? Can they see me?

The Bible tells me that those who trust in Jesus go to be with Him when they die. What does that mean?

What age is my child now? What do they look like?

When I see them again, will I recognize them?

What is heaven like? What will we be doing there? How does all this work?

The questions just keep coming. I feel like I need answers, but perhaps I don't.

God calls me to trust Him. If I had all the answers, there would be no reason to trust.

And yet, I wonder.

The death of a child throws our entire existence into a tailspin. Questions explode from somewhere deep within us. We wonder about a lot of things.

We might already have answers to some of our questions. Few of these answers, however, will be emotionally satisfying. Our child is no longer with us. Our hearts are naturally overwhelmed by this.

Though we get few satisfying answers, our hearts must still ask the questions. Finding ways to honestly express what's happening inside us is crucial on this grief journey. What we don't express remains inside us to surface again and again until we give it the attention it deserves.

Asking questions is part of honoring our child. Wondering is part of trying to find some resolution about what happened and why.

The Psalm writers peppered God with questions, especially during times of injustice, uncertainty, and personal suffering. They gave voice to what was happening in their hearts. They took their confusion, frustration, angst, and grief to God.

The Apostle Paul wrote, "We are confident, I say, and would prefer to be away from the body and at home with the Lord" (2 Cor. 5:8). Immediately after death, we are with Him—and more alive than we have ever been before. We will be with the One who knew us, wanted us, planned us, and created us. We will be home—truly, finally home.

We will also be truly, finally, and completely free. Free from sin. Free from pain, disease, temptation, and struggle. Free to be exactly who we were created to be, all the time.

God is gracious and kind to you. Be gracious and kind to yourself.

At present, however, we are not in heaven. We're here, and we're grieving. A glorious future may not take away the pain, but it can give great perspective to the pain.

"There will be no more death, or mourning, or crying, or pain, for the old order of things has passed away." Revelation 21:4

Lord, I give my questions and wonderings to You. I seek You. Give me more of an eternal perspective. I want to trust You more.

28

Where is God in all this?

Yes, I know He's with me. He's with everyone. He's everywhere. He can do anything. He cares for me.

I know all these things, but I don't feel them.

I wonder if I feel much of anything.

I'm still angry with Him. Or perhaps I just don't understand.

I know I'm holding back. I feel like I'm distancing my heart from Him. Either that or He's disappeared on me like everyone else.

I want to know why this happened. Why did my child have to die?

If God would tell me why, then perhaps I could let this go. Maybe then I could see some good that might come out of it.

Right now, I see nothing good in this at all.

Thank you for being honest and sharing your heart. Thank you for expressing your grief openly.

The pain of the loss of our child causes us to question many things, even God Himself. Many of us distance ourselves from God in our confusion and pain. We hunger to understand.

When we need to know something and can't seem to figure it out on our own, we ask an expert. God is the expert on all things, so we naturally bring our questions to Him.

If we sense silence, it hurts. We can feel like He doesn't care. As a result, we can feel more alone and even more devastated.

Keep being honest with Him. Though you might pull away from Him, He will never pull away from you.

Express your heart. Be real. Grieve.

Why, my soul, are you downcast? Why so disturbed within me? Put your hope in God, for I will yet praise Him, my Savior and my God.
Psalm 42:5

Lord, You feel far away. I'm angry, and I don't know what to think. I fear my heart is shutting down. Help.

29

All this has made me think of death more—a lot more.

My child died. Other children are going to die. I'm going to die. We're all going to die. None of us escapes this.

That's terrifying.

And it could happen anytime, anywhere, to anyone. After all, if this can happen, what else might?

I wonder if I'm getting paranoid. I don't feel like myself at all. I hate this fear.

Am I going crazy? I know I've asked that before.

My heart is shaking. I miss my child.

The loss of a child is shocking. This death brings many things home to us.

Perhaps we think of death more. We imagine what else might happen. Our own mortality and that of everyone around comes into sharp focus.

Suddenly uncertainty surrounds us. We're stunned by how little we control. The proverbial carpet has been pulled out from under us. We find ourselves wondering about almost everything. We tremble inside.

No, you're not crazy. Most grieving parents experience this.

You need reassurance. We all do. God is good at this. This is what His Word and His promises are all about.

He reassures us of who He is and who we are. He is our Shepherd. He provides and leads. He knows our fears. He meets us in our grief and pain. He never leaves us.

Breathe. You are not alone. You are not crazy. You're grieving for your child.

On my bed I remember you; I think of you through the watches of the night. Because you are my help, I sing in the shadow of your wings. I cling to you; your right hand upholds me.
Psalm 63:6-8

God, I'm terrified of what might happen next. I need Your reassurance. I cling to You.

30

I feel guilty.

I find myself thinking about what I should have said and could have done.

I regret things I said and did. I grieve over what I didn't say and didn't do.

I ask, "What if..." I wonder, "If only..."

The guilt is heavy. I feel terrible about myself. I feel like I'm coming apart. How could I let this happen?

I'm embarrassed and ashamed. I want to hide. I can't turn back the clock. I can't make any of this right.

My child is gone.

What do I do with this?

I feel like I'm punishing myself, and I can't seem to stop.

After the death of our child, we wonder about what we could have done and didn't, or what we did that we wish we hadn't. Regrets surface. Guilt invades. This is natural and common for grieving parents.

Yet, guilt is not our friend. Guilt only leads to shame. It produces nothing good. It keeps us looking at ourselves. Guilt boxes us in and then keeps us imprisoned.

Release yourself. If there are things you need to ask forgiveness for, do that. Confession is good for the soul. Receive God's forgiveness. His mercy and grace are always there, waiting for you.

Jesus Christ died for our sins. Our debt has been paid in full. It is finished. Nothing you have ever done, or could ever do or neglect to do, is stronger than Jesus' sacrifice for you.

His cross conquered your sin. He knows you. He forgives you. He releases you from guilt.

Think on this. See Jesus in front of you. Release feelings of guilt to Him. Walk into His arms and rest. His acceptance is perfect.

---

*Therefore, there is now no condemnation
for those who are in Christ Jesus.*
Romans 8:1

God, I release this guilt to You. If it returns, I'll release it again. I rest in Your acceptance and love.

31

I'm exhausted.

I'm still walking around in a fog. I can't think straight. My sleep isn't what it was. My energy level is way down.

I drag myself out of bed. I drag myself around and out. I drag myself through work and errands.

Everywhere I go, I feel alone – even in a crowd.

I drag myself back home. I stare at the walls. I blip out. Time passes, and I wonder where it went.

I'm tired all the time.

Is there something wrong with me? Am I sick?

Maybe I need to see a doctor.

My child is gone, and now it seems like I'm disappearing.

Fatigue is the number one physical symptom of grief, especially with the loss of a child. Your entire system is getting hit by this loss. After a while, your mind and body shift into maintenance mode. There is no energy for anything else.

When loss strikes, grief is the result. Grief enters our lives and takes up an enormous amount of space. Physical space. Mental space. Emotional space. Spiritual space. There's much less of us available to do routine life.

For most of us, normal life is demanding enough. The loss of a child throws a grenade into all this. This terrible loss stuns us and turns life upside down. Doing life takes way more energy than before.

There are times you will feel alone in all this—even though you're surrounded by people. Perhaps especially when surrounded by people.

Fatigue is the result. Exhaustion is natural and common for bereaved parents.

If you're concerned about your health, get checked out. Seeing a doctor during challenging times is always a good idea.

In the Bible, people in grief often expressed exhaustion. No wonder. We're wired for connection and created for relationship. As a parent, the loss of our child rattles us to the core. Sometimes, we can barely raise our heads.

Rest as best as you can. God can handle your life. Though you may not perceive it, He is at work in you. He is your life. Let Him be your life today.

The Lord is my shepherd, I lack nothing. He makes me lie down in green pastures, He leads me beside quiet waters, He refreshes my soul.
Psalm 23:1-2

Lord, I can barely lift my head. Restore and refresh me. Manage my routine. You are my Shepherd.

32

I guess everyone expects me to be over this.

Get over my child? That's ridiculous—and impossible.

Every time I mention my child, people grow quiet. They look uncomfortable. Fear comes into their eyes.

They change the subject. They excuse themselves and disappear.

And I'm left there, alone in my grief.

I sometimes wonder if anyone cares. I sense that some people are avoiding me altogether.

What do I do with that?

No one likes grief, I guess—especially this kind of grief.

Can't people see how badly I'm hurting? Can't they just accept me where I am?

You're right. The world doesn't like grief. People don't know what to do with it. Few people can handle being in the presence of intense suffering for long.

When the world encounters a grieving parent, it runs and hides. As a parent who has lost a child, your presence reminds them of the uncomfortable truth that anything can happen to anyone at any time. People don't want to acknowledge this, much less think about and engage with it.

We're made for relationships. We all experience terrible loss. We're designed to be loving and supportive of each other. Yet most of us choose personal comfort over meeting people where they are in their pain.

Thankfully, the Lord is an expert at this. He is well acquainted with loss, suffering, grief, and pain. For those who are willing, He can train them to be compassionate conveyors of His love and care.

You can be such a vessel—a reflection of His love, hope, and healing to this wounded world.

There are people out there who get it. They are safe and compassionate. Look for them. Ask God to bring them into your life.

I hope in the Lord Jesus to send Timothy to you soon, that I also may be cheered when I receive news about you. I have no one else like Him, who will show genuine concern for your welfare.
Philippians 2:19-20

Lord, I feel so alone now. Send me a few people like Timothy. Provide companions for me on this painful, confusing journey.

33

I'm having trouble finding supportive people.

I've gotten enough weird looks and blank stares. I expected kindness and compassion. Instead, people I counted on are disappearing before my eyes.

I'm keeping more to myself. I'm starting to pull back and grieve in private. This feels safer.

But I also feel alone – so alone. And angry.

I'm sad it's this way. Shouldn't it be different? Shouldn't we be loving and supportive to one another?

I try to trust, and then I get disappointed.

How do I know whom to share with and whom not to?

My heart is extremely fragile. Every interaction feels risky, even if nothing is said.

I miss my child.

If it helps any, what you're describing is common. Most grieving parents experience this. Most people don't know what to do with the intense grief that flows from the loss of a child.

We all need safe people in our lives. Safe people meet us where we are. They don't judge. They don't try to fix. They listen.

Safe people have no personal agenda for you or your life. Their only goal is to love you where you are, as you are.

In most cases, safe people are those who have known significant loss and pain, perhaps even the loss of a child. The Lord places these people around us, though we may not know them yet.

He invites us to trust Him with what we need. You need some safe people in your life. Ask the Lord to bring them to you. Ask Him to open your eyes to recognize them. Seek Him about this need.

He loves you. He is with you in this. He knows your pain and loneliness. He is providing for you.

So I say to you: Ask and it will be given to you; seek and you will find; knock and the door will be opened to you. For everyone who asks receives; the one who seeks finds; and to the one who knocks, the door will be opened.
Luke 11:9-10

Lord, bring safe people into my life. Lead me to them. I ask, seek, and knock.

34

Where are these safe people that you talk about?

It seems like everyone I encounter either runs away or tries to fix me.

How do you fix the loss of a child?

Where are the people who will listen? Where are those who will ask about my child and let me share?

My heart is full and burdened. I want to share, but I'm having trouble finding anyone I feel safe with.

Yes, a journal is good. Writing and talking out loud to myself help. But I need people too. I need hugs and touch amid all this.

I believe there are safe people out there. I want to find them.

What can I do?

Safe people are rare indeed, but they're out there.

I believe that God brings us the people we need—or brings us to them. He knows who and what we need.

Amid the pain and grief, we look up and seek. We ask for these people.

Provide for us, Lord.

I've found that the best way to find safe, supportive people is to become one myself. Safe, compassionate people are drawn to each other like magnets. They intuitively recognize one another.

In your grief, try focusing on being safe for others. Put aside judgment. Observe. Listen. Refrain from fixing. Enter their world and spend a few moments with them there.

The Lord will bless this. He will empower you. He can do this in and through you. As you do this, you'll sense His presence and love over time.

Do to others as you would have them do to you.
Luke 6:31

Lord, live through me and express Your love to others. I feel so empty, but You are limitless. Make me a safe person.

35

Sometimes, I seem to be doing better, and then I get hit again.

The grief comes and smacks me, seemingly out of nowhere.

A song. A familiar place. A picture. A certain aroma. A sudden memory.

Anything can set me off.

My child is everywhere and in everything. And yet, they're not here.

The grief wells up inside me so quickly. It feels like I'm going to burst if I don't let it out.

When this happens in public, I feel embarrassed, scared, and a little crazy. Is this normal?

I miss my child. They are never far from my mind.

What do I do with this?

Grief bursts. We all have them. For grieving parents, these sudden grief attacks can be intense and even debilitating.

We're minding our own business and something triggers memories and thoughts of our child. Grief falls upon us like an anvil. Anything can trigger us. Anytime. Anywhere.

This can lead us to live in fear, as if we're always walking on eggshells, waiting for the next grief attack. We shift from living to protecting ourselves. This is extremely common for grieving parents, and it can be so frustrating.

The reality is that your grief bursts honor your child. These sudden grief attacks proclaim how much you love and miss them.

When the grief hits, breathe. Breathe deeply and slowly. Remember the Lord is with you, right then, in that moment. You are in Christ, and He is in you.

God walks with you in your grief. He holds you every step of the way.

He feels your grief. Lean into Him. And breathe.

We wait in hope for the Lord; He is our help and our shield.
Psalm 33:20

Lord, I accept that grief bursts will come. When the emotion hits, cause me to look to You and rest in You. You are my shield. I am safe and secure in You.

36

I want to talk more about these grief bursts.

I'm scared. I dread the next one. It's embarrassing, and I feel out of control.

I'm pulling back more. My heart is going into hiding.

Is there a way I can prepare for grief bursts, even though I never know when they will happen or what will trigger them?

It seems I'm in fight-or-flight mode all the time. I fear I'm shutting down to try and keep myself under control.

I long for my child. I want my child back.

Fear can be such a large part of grief, especially when we lose a child. If we get hit enough, we start bracing for future blows rather than living in the present.

Yes, you can proactively prepare for grief bursts.

Imagine yourself in a public place and suddenly the grief strikes. What will you do? What are your options? What do you want to be able to do?

You could breathe deeply and make your way to someplace more private.

If you're talking to someone, you could excuse yourself.

You could breathe deeply where you are and see how you do.

There may be some cases where you can stay and continue on after a pause.

The key is to take your heart seriously and do what's best for you.

Ask the Lord for guidance in this. Go through it in your mind and decide beforehand how you will handle it.

You're right. Grief bursts will come. The Lord knows and is not surprised by them. He is with you in them. Decide with Him how you will approach them.

Again, please remember that grief bursts are natural and common for bereaved parents. Your grief attacks honor your child and express your love for them.

Guide me in your truth and teach me, for you are God my Savior, and my hope is in you all day long.
Psalm 25:5

God, I give my fear to You. Give me the ability to feel the fear and then let it pass on through. Guide and teach me.

37

I thought my family would understand.

I guess not.

Some are supportive. Others seem impatient.

They look at me with eyes that say, "Come on. Get over it. Move on."

Really? We're talking about my child here.

Get over it? What does that mean? How insensitive can a person be?

I had counted on family to be there for me. This is disappointing and painful.

This loss impacts them too. I don't understand why they're acting this way. Don't they care?

I know they love me, but most of them aren't helpful right now. I find myself hiding more when I'm with them.

I can't believe this is happening.

Shockingly, many grieving parents find family to be less than supportive. They're compassionate for a while, but if our grief lasts for more than a month, they wonder what's wrong with us.

This impacts us greatly. We long to be seen, heard, and understood, especially when we're in pain. Family should be the best and safest place to grieve openly and freely. Sadly, this is often not the case.

For the sake of our own hearts, we may need to lower our expectations of those around us, including family. Rather than risk growing bitter, it's best to forgive quickly, and then keep forgiving as necessary.

The Lord understands. He hears and knows your heart. Jesus' own family didn't understand Him, His mission, or why He did what He did.

You're in good company. Immerse yourself in Him. See yourself resting in Him.

For the sake of your own heart, forgive and release hurts and offenses. Jesus is an expert at this. He lives in you. Ask Him to work through you.

Be kind and merciful to each other, forgiving one another, just as God in Christ has forgiven you.
Ephesians 4:32

Lord, love my family through me. Protect my heart from hurt and damage. Enable me to be real and to forgive quickly when I'm disappointed.

38

Family members aren't the only ones who are less than supportive right now. I sense my coworkers are starting to roll their eyes.

They stop talking when I come near. I feel like I've got the plague or something.

I smile and fake it. It's easier this way.

I cry alone. My grief has become a private thing. I guess most people prefer it that way.

No wonder I feel alone in all this, even while surrounded by people that I know care about me. At least, I think they care about me.

I find myself being sarcastic and morose, but I try to hide that too. I'm talking to myself most of the time. I don't trust anyone else to listen.

Why did my child have to die?

This is so, so hard.

Good listeners can be hard to find at times. Although we all know grief, few people process it well. We tend to shove our grief down deep inside, only to have it leak out in anger, frustration, anxiety, and depression.

This is especially true when we lose a child.

Keep breathing deeply. Keep finding ways to express your pain and grief. Write it out. Talk it out—even out loud to yourself. Draw or paint it out. Exercise it out.

The workplace is notorious for ignoring grief. Performance is expected. Work colleagues will be compassionate and supportive at first, but that quickly fades into the background because, "We have work to do."

The Lord is with you at work. He goes before you. He sits with you and walks with you. He lives in you, and He is always working. He is your constant companion.

See Him at your workplace. Talk to Him. Unload the pain and frustration to Him. Embrace His companionship.

Forgive and release offenses quickly. Allow Jesus to do this in and through you. You don't need any extra burdens right now. Guard your heart.

Hannah replied, "I am a woman who is deeply troubled...I was pouring out my soul to the Lord...I have been praying here out of my great anguish and grief."
1 Samuel 1:15-16

Lord, You are my strength. Live through me and empower me to do all You call me to. Let me see You in my work.

39

I'm alive, but some days I feel like I'm barely here.

I go through the motions. I get up. I move. I go where I'm supposed to and do some of what I'm expected to do.

I interact. I have conversations. I even smile now and then.

Inside, I feel alone and lost. Numb. Empty.

I'm just existing.

Sometimes I wonder if I've lost my own heart. I can't feel it anymore. Either that or I'm overwhelmed with feelings.

I wonder if I'll explode one day—or implode.

I'm embarrassed. I'm a person of faith, but that doesn't seem to be making much of a difference right now.

"I'm just existing." This is a common statement among grieving parents.

Everything has changed. All of life has shifted. Some routine parts of life have disappeared. Many expectations and dreams have disintegrated overnight.

The loss of our child takes over our minds and hearts. It seems we can think of nothing else. We live in two worlds—our own world of grief and the outside world that speeds on ahead as if nothing has happened.

Broken Walk

The sheer emotional intensity drains us. We live in a fog. We feel like shadows of our former selves. Our lives become mechanical, even robotic.

In Proverbs, King Solomon said, "Above all else, guard your heart, for it is the spring from which everything else in life flows." Our hearts are getting pummeled. We must find ways to protect and nurture our hearts as we hurt, grieve, and mourn.

We share our grief with God. He knows our grief already, but He longs for us to express our hearts to Him. He knows we need this.

Some pray out loud because this helps "get the grief out". We get to hear our own voices in the process, which is more important than we realize.

As we walk with the Lord—seeking Him and digesting His word—He will comfort our souls. He is our comfort, our peace, our life. Even though we're "just existing" at present, God is at work healing us from the inside out.

Now is not forever. Present yourself to your heavenly Father again today. Release all to Him.

Let the morning bring me word of your unfailing love, for I have put my trust in you. Show me the way I should go, for to you I entrust my life.
Psalm 143:8

Lord, I trust that You are at work in me. I feel like a shell of my former self. Bring healing over time. Restore my soul. Empower me to walk closely with You today.

40

I seem to be forgetting things more. Where I put stuff. Why I came into the room. What I was doing. Where I was going.

I forget appointments. I can't remember what day it is. It's like my brain is going numb.

This is scary. What's happening to me? Is this grief?

Of course, I imagine the worst.

Do I have a brain tumor? Mental illness? Dementia?

My child is gone and is not coming back. This is all more than I can bear.

I'm starting to worry—about myself, about everything.

Is this ever going to get better? Do I even want it to get better?

I want my child back.

Grief from the death of a child hits a parent with incredible force. The mental and cognitive effects can be disturbing.

Perhaps you can't focus or concentrate. You forget things. Maybe you blip out at times. Grieving moms and dads often go blank and stare at walls.

This is natural and common for bereaved parents. You are a closed system. You have only so much mental space. When deep grief like this invades, it gobbles up a lot of mental real estate.

Simply put, you have less brain available for everyday functioning. The result is usually increased forgetfulness and decreased mental energy and focus.

As you continue to process the grief inside you, these mental challenges will most likely improve over time.

Lay these things before the Lord. Express your fears, doubts, and concerns. He is listening. He is protecting you and providing for you, even if you don't feel His presence.

You are completely dependent on Him today. We all are. He is faithful. He is at work in you and for you every moment.

Rest in Him. He is working for your good.

That is why, for Christ's sake, I delight in weaknesses, in insults, in hardships, in persecutions, in difficulties. For when I am weak, then I am strong.
2 Corinthians 12:10

Lord, even though I feel like I'm falling apart, You are at work in and through me. I am loved. I am safe and secure. You know my heart. I rest in You.

41

A new shock wave hit me yesterday.

I went into my child's room. Grief smacked me like a tsunami.

Everything I laid my eyes on brought up a memory. The pain was immense.

What am I going to do with all this?

Keep a few special things and then give the rest away?

Let other family and friends have some things?

Keep everything?

Right now, I can't bear the thought of parting with anything. I know these possessions are not my child, but they are all I have left.

It's too much to contemplate. Too much for now.

When I left the room, I started to close the door. I decided to leave it open.

I don't know what to do.

As people of faith, we can tell ourselves that possessions don't matter. They are merely things. When a child dies, their things become an extension of them.

For now, our child's possessions represent our child. It's natural, therefore, to want to hang on to anything and everything that reminds us of them. Their presence lingers in clothes, objects, and pictures.

There will come a time to decide what to do with your child's possessions. You don't need to force this. As you seek the Lord about this, He will guide you. You will know when it is time.

God often shares His wisdom with us through other people. We tend to try to figure things out on our own. Sometimes it's a challenge to wait for the Lord and to stay open.

There is no hurry. You can take your time. Grief has a timing to it. Don't worry about getting it just right. Rather, simply seek the Lord and walk with Him as best you know how.

As you continue to give yourself and your pain to Him, the next step will become visible at the proper time.

You do not need to fear your grief. Yes, at times it is overwhelming. Let it come. Express what's happening inside you. See Jesus in it with you, because He is.

Lay all in His hands. He suffered and died for you. He knows your pain. He is the ultimate grief expert.

Turn your ear to me, come quickly to my rescue; be my rock of refuge, a strong fortress to save me. Since you are my rock and my fortress, for the sake of your name lead and guide me.
Psalm 31:2-3

Lord, I give myself to You again today. I release my worries and fears to You. I release trying to figure things out. Help me to seek, to wait, and to walk closely with You.

42

We were a family. What are we now?

I mean, yes, we're still a family. But with one missing, everything feels different, wrong, and broken.

Broken—that's the right word. Our family is broken now.

Our family has changed—and is changing. I can feel it.

One of us is gone. Who are we now? What will we be? How does all this work?

Gone does not mean forgotten. We will never forget. I can't forget.

Just because my child is gone doesn't mean they are no longer a part of this family.

We miss them. We love them. We will, must, find ways to include them.

Somehow. Someway.

Biological or adopted, our children are a part of us. After the death of a child, we find ourselves thrust into a strange, new world. Our child is no longer physically present, but they are still fully present in our minds and hearts.

Our child is now the proverbial elephant in every room. It is this way for every member of our immediate family, whether they admit it or not. Our child's absence permeates the atmosphere we breathe.

We must acknowledge and embrace this elephant. We boldly speak our child's name. We talk about them. We share memories. We remember. We honor them with our grief.

Perhaps not everyone in our family wants to talk about the one who is missing. This is natural. Who wants to feel pain? And yet, the pain still resides in us and will eventually work itself out into our lives and relationships, usually in ways that create distress.

God personally knits children together in their mother's wombs. They are special and priceless. God sets us in families. Each one of us is unique. When one member departs, all the others feel the pain in their own way.

God invites us to share our pain. He counsels us to look up and trust Him for guidance through this huge, deep valley of grief. He offers to bring comfort and healing to each heart in His own time and way.

Lay your family before Him. Give your family to Him. He knows each person completely—body, soul, and spirit. He is your heavenly Father, who is ready and willing to pilot each of you through this current wilderness.

You, God, are my God, earnestly I seek you; I thirst for you, my whole being longs for you in a dry and parched land where there is no water.
Psalm 63:1

Lord, I give myself and my family to You. We are brokenhearted. Bring Your comfort and healing to each of us. Move each of our hearts to seek You through this painful time.

43

I had a panic attack today.

A cloud of anxiety came upon me at work. My heart raced. I felt lightheaded. My vision narrowed.

Everything closed in on me. I started hyperventilating. The panic I felt was awful.

I sat for a moment, and then began breathing deeply.

It took a while, but I finally stood up and went to the restroom to collect myself. I decided I needed to step outside for a moment. I felt claustrophobic.

It was terrifying. I thought I was dying.

I'm worried. I can't be having episodes like this. I'm scared I won't be able to function.

What's happening to me? I feel like I'm coming apart.

Yes, that sounds like a panic attack. As you said, such attacks are terrifying.

When we lose a child, our hearts are stunned, and our anxiety level naturally skyrockets. Emotion takes over.

Over time, the grief and anxiety can build to a point where a panic attack occurs.

Most people who have a panic attack almost immediately begin to fear the next one. Of course, that doesn't help matters any.

Don't try to fight the anxiety or keep the panic from coming. This only focuses your mind even more on the anxiety itself. Instead, try to view the panic attack as a release of all your pent-up anxiety, worry, fear, and grief.

If you feel a panic attack coming, breathe. Breathe slowly and deeply—in through the nose and out through the mouth. You can let the panic pass on through rather than holding on to it and letting it take over.

As you breathe deeply, pray. "Lord, I know you're in this with me. I'm anxious. I'll breathe and let You handle this."

Be kind to yourself. Be patient with yourself. Your child is gone from your sight. This is monstrously hard.

Do not be anxious about anything, but pray about everything, making your requests to God with thanksgiving. And then the peace of God, which is beyond all understanding, will guard your hearts and minds in Christ Jesus.
Philippians 4:5-6

Lord, You are my peace. I release my anxious thoughts to You. You will lead me through this dark valley. You are my constant companion.

44

I think I'm doing a little better, and then I'm not.

It seems like I'm making tiny bits of progress, then I wonder if I've made any progress at all. Two steps forward. Three steps back.

I have a few moments when the pain recedes into the background. The next moment, I'm non-functional. My emotions are volatile and unpredictable.

This is discouraging. I feel like I'm constantly swimming upstream and against the current. Daily life takes so much more energy now.

And I feel like I'm doing this alone.

My resiliency is gone. I'm not bouncing back. I'm exhausted.

My child is never far from my mind. My child is a part of me, yet they are not here.

What do I do with that?

It's hard to measure progress in grief after a traumatic loss like this. Grief is not a straight road, but rather more like a winding path strewn with rocks, holes, twigs, and the occasional log. At times, you can't see the path at all. You're in uncharted territory.

Feeling lost is natural because you don't really know where you are. You know what life was, but not what it is and will be.

You're adjusting to what happened— to the loss of your precious child.

This grief journey is arduous and takes time. You can feel like you're on a treadmill going nowhere.

However, if you're trusting the Lord as best you can and processing your grief in healthy ways, you're slowly healing, no matter how it might seem.

Life can only be lived one moment at a time. The grief path can only be walked one step at a time.

Immerse yourself in God's Word. Listen as you read. Hear the voice of your shepherd. He is here. He is at work. He is working for you, in you.

***Surely your goodness and love will follow
me all the days of my life, and I will dwell
in the house of the Lord forever.
Psalm 23:6***

Lord, my world is upside down. You, however, have not changed. Your goodness and love follow me everywhere, even though I may not feel this. Cause me to trust You.

45

There are some mean people out there.

*They might sound nice and seem helpful,
but in the end, they're mean.*

They don't see or hear me. They judge. They evaluate.

*Apparently, I don't measure up. They tell me how
to fix myself because I'm the problem.*

Then they walk away and don't lift a finger to help.

I want to scream, "What do you expect? I've lost my child!"

*Yes, I'm angry today. I'm a bit jaded about humanity.
I'm growing more reluctant to trust anyone. My
heart can't handle any more beatings.*

*What gives them the right to say these things?
Who do they think they are?*

Breathe. I need to breathe.

You're right.

We meet different kinds of people in grief. Sounds like you've been exposed to some hyper-critical judges.

They evaluate others but not themselves. They push their own issues off on others. They hide behind their platitudes. They are fixers and unsolicited advice-givers. They deliver their edicts and then disappear, only to reappear later to check how well you're following what they told you to do. To keep their own struggles at bay, they point out yours.

I've had plenty of experience with these folks too. Most grieving parents have. Toxic judges are not friends of your heart. Avoid them.

If you can't avoid them, guard your heart and limit their influence. Far from helpful, their words and behavior are destructive. Love them and yourself by limiting your exposure to them.

As the hyper-critical judges spout their edicts, see the Lord with you in that moment. Hear Him whisper, "I love you."

Far from tossing you platitudes, God enters your grief and walks with you there.

Breathe deeply. Know that He is with you, in you. He invites you to rest in Him.

But you, Lord, do not be far from me. You are my strength; come quickly to help me.
Psalm 22:19

God, lead me to helpful, supportive people. Enable me to forgive offenses quickly so that the critical judgments of others do not rule my heart. Work through me, Lord.

46

I feel so sad.

My sadness is a cloud that surrounds me. Some days everything seems sad. All of life is colored by this loss.

I miss my child.

I miss their voice and their presence. On days like this, I miss everything.

Part of the sadness feels good because it feels right. I should be sad.

Then part of me feels guilty. I should be happy for my child. I should be rejoicing that they are with the Lord and more alive than ever before.

I feel so divided and confused sometimes.

Sadness can be so heavy. I'm seeing everything through sad lenses today.

My world is dull and drab. Everything seems colorless.

Sadness is natural, appropriate, and healthy. Your child died. Your heart aches. You love your child and want to be together.

God made us for relationship. Separation, even temporary separation, is painful. Sadness is a natural result.

Pour your sadness out before the Lord. Express your heart to Him. He is the best listener in the universe.

He knows all about sadness. He sits with you in this heavy cloud of grief. He knows and understands your heart. He lives in you.

Breathe. Openly acknowledge the sadness. Embrace it. Your heart is expressing your love for your child.

---

*You are my refuge and my shield; I
have put my hope in your word.
Psalm 119:114*

*Lord, You feel my sadness. I live in You, my
refuge. You are my hope and my life.*

47

Though time has passed, I'm back to having trouble fathoming all this.

How can my child be gone?

It's all so strange. I guess my mind doesn't want to accept it. My heart is having trouble too.

I want my child back. I want my child here—now.

I want to see their smile, hear their voice, and experience their presence.

It's like I woke up one day in another world -- an alternate universe – and I've been living there ever since.

I keep expecting to wake up and discover this was all a bad dream.

God created us in His image and made us for relationship—with Him and with other people. When physical ties are severed, especially when that tie is our child, our hearts shake. Our minds scream, "No!"

This should not be. Something about it seems wrong. Life feels weird. Surreal.

When a child dies, everything feels wrong, off, and strange. Love doesn't disappear, however. It endures. It lasts. It runs deep and reaches past this life.

You love your child. Your heart longs to express your love. This is natural and healthy.

Find ways to express your love for your child. Write a letter. Journal. Draw. Express your affection.

Be honest with God in all this. Share with Him how you long to be with your child again. He already knows your heart, but He delights in hearing the voice of your heart.

God loves you. You are His child.

> ***When I said, "My foot is slipping," your unfailing love, Lord, supported me.***
> ***Psalm 94:18***

God, my world has changed, but You have not. Guide me to grieve well and to express my love for my child.

48

Since my child's death, every day seems like a trip through the past.

It's as if my child's life is flashing before my eyes. I get glimpses—images and mental videos of them through their life. One after the other, the memories come.

I cry. Sometimes I sob. Other times, there are no tears left.

I sit and hang my head. I wonder all over again how this happened and why.

The images in my head can drive me wild with sadness and longing. Part of me wants this mental loop of memories to stop. Another part of me wants to just sit there, hour after hour, watching them over and over again.

It's like my child is still here, even though they're gone. Or perhaps I just don't want my child to be gone. Maybe I'm hanging on to them any way I can.

Is this normal?

Sometimes I think I'm losing it. Maybe I am.

I feel like I'm going around and around, stuck in a perpetual grief loop.

Our hearts are memory collectors. What comes in through our eyes, ears, and other senses gets cataloged and placed in its appropriate box. Our memory boxes get stored in our memory warehouse.

Of course, some memories are more powerful and influential than others. Given the right stimulus, decades-old recollections can spill forth in an instant.

When a child dies, some of our memory boxes burst open. Our child's life truly does begin to flash before our eyes.

When these memory flashes come, embrace them. Your heart is speaking. Feel the emotions that come with them. If you can, try talking out loud. Express what you're thinking and feeling.

You can even be proactive and open your mental memory boxes intentionally. Sit down and write about a particular recollection involving your child. Write honestly without editing. Get down on paper (or on a screen) what's happening inside you at the moment.

All this is part of "getting the grief out". It's also part of honoring your child and the Lord who created them. You are guarding and nurturing your own heart at the same time.

The Lord knows all that is in your mind and heart. He knows the content of each memory box perfectly. Give every aspect of your grief journey to Him. Pour out to Him your sadness, anger, guilt, confusion, and longing.

Talk with Him about everything.

Where can I go from Your Spirit? Where can I flee from Your presence? If I go up to the heavens, You are there; if I make my bed in the depths, You are there. Psalm 139:7-8

Lord, help me to embrace the memories and feel the emotions. Remind me that You are there—here—with me, all the time. I give myself and this painful journey to You.

49

I'm trying to focus on using my sadness to express my love for my child and to thank God for them.

I'm giving myself permission to be sad but using my sadness for good. This feels good and right.

Love. Yes, it's about love. I want to keep expressing my love for my child and find more ways to do that.

Somehow, I think that might help the intense pain of missing them.

I will always miss them. That's okay. It's about love.

My grief proclaims my love, doesn't it?

Yes, it does. You love, and so you grieve.

Using your grief to express love for your child is wonderful and healing.

Yes, it's about love. And yes, you will always miss them. How could you not? That's natural, and healthy.

Be creative and find more ways to express your love for your child. When you do, you're also expressing love for God who created them. You can even turn that around and focus on expressing love for Him by grieving well and honoring your child.

When asked what the greatest commandment was, Jesus said,

"Love the Lord your God with all your heart and with all your soul and with all your strength and with all your mind; and love your neighbor as yourself."

Love God. Love people. Loving God leads to loving people.

Jesus loved (and loves) your child. He will express that love for your child through you as their earthly parent. Your grief can be a part of this.

When we use our grief to fuel gratitude, good things happen. Our hearts heal a bit. Our souls begin to settle a little.

When love for your child is expressed, God is honored.

For God so loved the world that he gave His one and only Son, that whoever believes in Him shall not perish but have eternal life.
John 3:16

My grief has purpose. I am expressing love. Lord, You are love. You live in me. Help me to do this well.

50

I've decided to focus on gratitude today.

The loss of my child is incredibly painful, but that doesn't mean I can't be thankful.

I'm thankful for my child. I thank God that He planned and created them. They were one of a kind, unique. God did that.

God gave them to me and me to them. He placed us in each other's lives.

God did so much for us and through us while we had each other. He gave us wonderful seasons together and led us through extremely difficult times.

I have lost much, but I have much to be thankful for. I didn't engineer any of that. It was all given to me.

I am blessed.

Questions still swirl around inside me, but for today I will focus on being thankful for what I had and what I have.

God can use gratitude to heal us. Choosing to be grateful is part of loving God and following Him.

When we give thanks for what God has done, God Himself is at work in and through us. God can use gratitude to turn the tables on depression and give our hearts a more eternal perspective.

God tells us to set our minds on the things above. We are told to fix our thoughts on Jesus. Gratitude is a huge part of this.

Thankfulness comforts the heart. When we choose to take off the glasses of loss and replace them with the lenses of gratitude, our outlook changes. We see more of the bigger picture.

A child is a gift from God. By definition, a gift is given freely and cannot be earned. Gifts are given in love.

God also gives us is the gift of memory. Right now, memories of your child might bring only tears. As you move through the grief, you will begin to smile through the tears as you think of them. Eventually, gratitude for your child will begin to dominate your heart.

Thankfulness is a wonderful way to honor God and love those who are no longer here—especially our children.

God is an amazing gift-giver. God delights in your thankfulness. He created you. He loves you perfectly.

Rejoice always. Pray continually. Give thanks in everything, for this is God's will for you in Christ Jesus.
1 Thessalonians 5:16-18

Lord, thank you. You have blessed me in extraordinary ways. Fill me with thankfulness, even amid this great grief.

51

*I looked at a calendar yesterday and winced.
In fact, I nearly collapsed.*

*I suddenly realized that my child will not be here
on my birthday—or Mother's Day, Father's Day,
Thanksgiving, Christmas, Valentine's Day, or Easter.*

*They won't be here at any graduations,
weddings, births, or special events.*

*It's like my calendar—my idea of the future—became a big,
blurry mass and then slowly evaporated before my eyes.*

The future is gone.

I was stunned all over again. I could hardly breathe.

*I found myself shouting and screaming. The sudden cascade of
sadness, anger, and bitter disappointment was overwhelming.*

*Every part of the future is affected. My future—my
family's future—is completely different now.*

How do I even think about this?

You're right. When we lose a child, the future changes.

What we had planned on and anticipated has been severely altered. It's as if part of our picture of what's down the road has been erased.

When we realize this, we become hyper-aware of the important events and occasions our child won't be here for. Their departure had a massive impact, the ripple effects go on and on.

We grieve about days that aren't even here yet. We mourn deeply in advance. All this is natural and common for bereaved parents.

This loss does indeed change everything because it changes us. But that doesn't mean that we can't heal, grow, and find ways to use these holidays and special times to honor our child and the Lord who created them.

The future is in God's hands. He has given many precious and powerful promises. He does what He says. Through faith in Jesus Christ, we have a grand and glorious future ahead.

Loss reminds us that this world is not our home. The Lord reminds us in His word that we are sojourners here. We occupy a particular place for a certain season. We are here on assignment for a period of time.

When the pain of missing our child strikes, we can remind ourselves of our soon and coming future with the Lord. God can bring an eternal perspective to our pain—and our view of the future.

---

*For the Lord himself will come down from heaven,
with a loud command, with the voice of the
archangel and with the trumpet call of God,
and the dead in Christ will rise first.
After that, we who are still alive and are left
will be caught up together with them in the clouds to
meet the Lord in the air.
And so we will be with the Lord forever.
Therefore encourage one another with these words.
1 Thessalonians 4:16-18*

Lord, I am grieving the future I had expected. I release my expectations, hopes, and dreams to you. Speak to me through Your word and remind me of the glories that are to come.

52

*I've discovered that some fellow believers will
be supportive, but others won't be.*

*I naturally expected people at church to understand,
but perhaps that was unrealistic. Until I experienced
this terrible loss myself, I didn't have a clue.*

*I admit I was less than compassionate and supportive to
those who were grieving. When I encountered someone who
had lost a child, I ran in the other direction. I immediately
thought of myself and how awful that would be.*

Now, it's happened to me.

*When someone says something unhelpful, I try to
be patient, but my initial reactions are powerful.
Emotion surges up in me so quickly.*

I have to tell myself, "Be quiet. Breathe."

I walk away hurt. I feel unseen, belittled, and more alone.

*I want to talk about my child.
Can't people understand that?*

Of course, you want to talk about your child. You love them. They're priceless and special. Your heart is overflowing with both grief and gratitude.

And you're right again. People who haven't been through this deep, soul-wrenching loss can't relate. They might sympathize for a little while, but they have trouble empathizing.

At first, we naturally expect other believers to be kind, supportive, and understanding, but they will not always be so. Our hearts are eager to share. We want to be able to trust.

Your heart is vulnerable right now, and whom you choose to trust is more important than ever. You need wisdom from the Lord about this.

Keep asking the Lord for those safe, trustworthy people. Keep sharing openly and honestly with Him.

He will always welcome you. He is always listening.

The Lord is gracious and compassionate, slow to anger and rich in love. The Lord is good to all; He has compassion on all He has made.
Psalm 145:8-9

Lord, make me loving, patient, and accepting, even in the face of unhelpful, judgmental comments. Love the speaker through me. I will forgive and release quickly. I want to honor my child, and You.

53

I find myself asking uncomfortable questions.
Did God take my child from me?
If God didn't take them, why did He allow this?
Why didn't He just heal them instead?
Couldn't we have had more time? Why then? Why that way?
Today, I can't see any good in what happened.
If that's true, then is God really good?
I'm scared to even entertain these thoughts. I feel ashamed.
Yet, my heart keeps coming back around to them. I have questions.
And if I allow myself to think about it, more questions surface.
What do I do with all this?

Loss generates questions, especially the loss of a child. This is natural and common.

Silencing our hearts by shoving uncomfortable questions aside is not the answer. Unexpressed and unprocessed questions tend to turn toxic. Seeds of debilitating doubt, anger, and bitterness can begin to grow.

God is not threatened by our questions. He knows your heart. He knows all your questions already. He invites you to express them honestly to Him.

Consider writing your questions down. See them on the page in front of you. Present them to the Lord.

Keep expressing your questions as they come, over and over if necessary. The Lord loves you. He is listening.

You may not get answers to some of your questions. If we understood everything, there would be no need for faith and trust. God invites you to trust Him with all that you don't understand.

Acknowledge those internal questions and express them openly to the Lord. Release them to Him as often as they surface. Immerse yourself in His word. Allow Him to speak to you.

"Praise be to the name of God for ever and ever; wisdom and power are His. He changes times and seasons; He deposes kings and raises up others. He gives wisdom to the wise and knowledge to the discerning. He reveals deep and hidden things; He knows what lies in darkness, and light dwells with Him."
Daniel 2:20-22

God, I give my questions to You, one by one. Teach me. I trust that You will make clear what You wish to, over time.

54

*I am trying to be honest with God about
the questions roaming in my heart.*

*I wrote them down and laid them before Him. There was
something about seeing them on the page that humbled me.*

*I realized that these questions are natural. My
heart wants answers. I want to know why.*

*Even as I say that, I know that God isn't obligated to
explain all this. I know there are other questions I will
never know the answers to until I'm in heaven.*

And then, perhaps all my questions will simply evaporate.

*I don't know what else to do, so I'll keep sharing
with God what's in my heart. After all, He already
knows my every thought and feeling.*

My heart aches. I miss my child.

We long to understand, yet we know this life is a walk of faith. Faith calls for us to trust amid all kinds of uncertainty.

In the end, I'm not sure there would be many emotionally satisfying answers to our questions about the loss of our children. Yet, we must ask. Our hearts are shaking and need reassurance.

When you find yourself wondering why, ask the question, and then return to what you know to be true.

God welcomes questions. None of us ever trusts Him perfectly. Our faith is mixed with fear, doubt, and wondering.

Jesus meets you where you are, as you are, and loves you there. He will guide you in this. He is good. His love endures forever.

"'If you can?" said Jesus. "Everything is possible for one who believes." Immediately the boy's father exclaimed, "I do believe; help me overcome my unbelief!"
Mark 9:23-24

Lord, I trust You. Deepen my trust. You know my questions. More than wanting answers, I want to know You.

55

I want to share my grief, my questions, and my struggles with others. I want their input and feedback. I need their support and love.

Sadly, most of the time I get blank stares and platitudes.

Losing my child was and is devastating. I'm in nonstop anguish at times. Why can't people just meet me where I am for even just a few moments?

I'm talking about people of faith too. I share a little and then get those phrases we've all heard a thousand times with God mixed into them.

Some quote Scripture to me. I feel like they're saying, "I don't have time for this. Here's a spiritual band-aid."

I know they mean well. At least, I think they do.

Perhaps it's unfair of me to share and involve them in my grief. But they look concerned and ask how I am. I share and walk away hurt and disappointed.

*When animals get hurt, they withdraw.
I understand that now.*

Well-meaning people can say some unhelpful things. They don't know what to do with our pain and grief, so they throw a few words at us and then walk away.

It would be easier if they told us, "I'm concerned about you, but I don't know what to do with your pain." Instead, they try to be nice. Bereaved parents are left feeling disappointed, alone, and socially unacceptable.

Worse yet, we can begin to feel that something's wrong with us.

Your heart is worth guarding. Try giving brief but honest answers to the questions of others. If they want to know more, they'll ask.

Release and forgive those who offend you—and quickly. Your heart doesn't need any extra burdens right now.

This is hard—and that's an understatement. Jesus, who lives in you, is an expert at doing hard things. He can empower you for this. He is with you in each and every interaction.

Keep asking God for wisdom. He lives in you. He will teach and guide you in this.

My relatives have gone away; my closest friends have forgotten me.
Job 19:14

People often don't understand, but You do. I release my frustration, pain, and anger to You, Lord. Lift my heart.

56

I'm having headaches lately. And stomach distress.

I'm tired all the time. I'm not sleeping well.

It feels like I'm always on the verge of getting sick.

Is grief taking its toll on my body too?

I move through the days with less energy. I feel like I'm just going through the motions. I feel frustrated and confused.

From the moment my child died, I started to disappear. I feel like a shadow of my former self.

Now, even my body is betraying me.

When we lose a child, grief hits our entire being. It affects us emotionally, mentally, spiritually, and physically.

Grief is a form of stress. Over time, it can suppress our immune system. We can begin having all sorts of physical symptoms—headaches, stomach distress, palpitations, panic attacks, raised blood pressure, aches and pains, etc.

This is not surprising. We're wired for relationship. Death and separation create great stress—especially when it involves a child (no matter how old).

We're parents. We'll always be parents, even if our children are gone from our sight. Our hearts wrestle with this deeply personal loss. Our minds try desperately to make sense of things.

No wonder you feel as you do. No wonder you're experiencing physical distress. Your child is a part of you. You feel their absence in your body too.

If you're concerned about your health, please see a physician. Make sure you tell them about the traumatic loss you're enduring. Breathe deeply. Take your health seriously.

Downgrade your expectations of yourself. Rest in the Lord. God can handle this. Release burdens and fears to Him.

Seek to do only what He puts on your plate today.

My life is consumed by anguish and my years by groaning; my strength fails because of my affliction, and my bones grow weak.
Psalm 31:10

Lord, You know what's happening inside me. Heal me. Give me wisdom to know what to do. You are my peace.

57

I've said before that I felt like I wasn't really living but just going through the motions.

I feel foggy. Tired. Numb.

Numb. That's it.

I'm one big ball of emotion, but I can't seem to feel it.

I look around and watch the world speeding along. I'm a part of it, but I can't seem to enter in.

My child is gone. My old life has disappeared. I feel like I'm disappearing.

I'm dazed. Stunned. Exhausted.

I sit and stare at the walls. I drive and forget where I'm going. I have conversations, but I'm not all there.

I don't like this. I'm afraid my heart is shutting down.

There comes a time in our grief process where most of us feel numb. Our hearts have been trying to manage all the emotions swirling around in us. Our minds have been active, desperately working through what has happened and all that it means. Perhaps our souls have been shaken.

The loss of our child has upended everything. No wonder we're dazed, sad, angry, anxious, fatigued, confused, and depressed.

At some point, our system needs a break. Our feelers shut down. Our minds go on autopilot. We begin to function on energy-save mode.

Feeling numb is common and natural in grief—especially after the loss of a child. Usually, it's a temporary rest stop on our grief journey.

Breathe. Accept yourself where you are. The Lord is at work in you and for you, even though you might not feel or perceive this. He is carrying you. Receive His love and care for you.

Now is not forever. Though it may be hard to imagine, your grief will change over time.

My heart is broken within me; all my bones tremble.
Jeremiah 23:9

Lord, You are my life. My hope is in You. Support me now. Hold me up. Remind me of Your love.

58

I'm beyond sadness. I feel depressed.

My child is gone. The color has been sucked out of my life.

Nothing looks good, sounds good, or tastes good.

I lie in bed in the morning and don't want to get up. I drag myself through the day. I put up my façade and focus on getting through the time without drawing too much attention or embarrassing myself too badly.

My heart is exhausted. I'm a shell. I feel empty.

The loneliness is exhausting.

I miss my child desperately.

Grief from the loss of a child is truly exhausting. This unwanted journey takes enormous energy.

You're enduring the unthinkable. Your child is gone. Your life has been upended, perhaps even shattered. All the change is overwhelming. Change is demanding, stressful, and incredibly exhausting— especially change you didn't want.

Most grieving parents experience some depression. As believers in Christ, we tend to hide this. We're embarrassed, even ashamed. We feel like we've failed. We tell ourselves that we are people of faith and should be stronger than this.

Job, Hannah, Naomi, David, Elijah, Jeremiah, and other biblical characters wrestled with depression at times. You're in good company. You're human. You're finite and limited.

Be honest with God about all this. He knows already. He loves you. He wants to hear your voice expressing your heart to Him.

Even now, He is at work in you. He is your constant companion. He loves you where you are, as you are.

You who are my Comforter in sorrow,
my heart is faint within me.
Jeremiah 8:18

Lord, You are my Comforter. I lay my numb and shattered heart in Your hands. Work in me. Restore me. You are my hope.

59

I feel like I'm going in circles. My heart hurts.

My head is heavy. My mind is never still.

My emotions are overwhelming. My relationships are strange.

I'm drained. Exhausted. I feel weak, vulnerable, and paralyzed.

Keeping my mask in place takes an incredible amount of energy. I have to find people that I can be real with.

I need to find someone who will listen. I need perspective. I need an objective voice in my life.

How do I find someone like this?

None of us can do this alone. We weren't meant to. We're designed for relationships and connection. We need each other, especially now.

For many grieving parents, we need more than just the support of family and friends. We need people who know loss—other souls who are well acquainted with grief. We need wise, safe people who can give us perspective and reassurance.

The loss of a child often creates tunnel vision. The intense pain directs all our attention to our child and their death. Over time, we need to begin to see this tragedy within the larger picture of life and eternity. Many times, an objective, outside voice can help us do that.

A mentor who knows grief well can speak to our hearts with knowledge, compassion, and sensitivity. A counselor or grief professional can be a safe listening ear and an excellent sounding board.

Reaching out for such help can be scary. We've been wounded deeply. Taking the risk to trust someone new can be unnerving.

The best things in life are often scary at first. Good things usually require great courage. God invites us to ask Him to provide what and who we need.

Is it time for you to pray about reaching out for support and input like this? Yes, God Himself is our ultimate counselor, but He often provides for us through other people. This blesses all of us.

God gifted us to minister to one another. We need each other.

Lay your heart and soul before the Lord. Yield yourself to His will. Trust Him to teach you and guide you. Be open to His answers.

Finally, all of you, be like-minded, be sympathetic, love one another, be compassionate and humble.
1 Peter 3:8

Lord, provide a grief mentor for me. Let me know what I need to do. You know who and what I need. I give myself to You again today. I release fear and worry to You.

60

I feel better today, and I think I know why.

A coworker asked me to lunch. While we were waiting for our food, they asked me how I was doing and added, "Yes, I really want to know."

I blinked. I started talking.

I stopped at points and looked them in the eye. They were still listening.

I talked on and on.

The food came, and I kept talking. Words poured out of me like water.

When we arrived back at work, I felt lighter—like someone had pushed a button and released some pressure. It felt good.

I need to talk. I need to let it out.

I need to talk about my child.

Part of being created in the image of God and designed for relationship is that all of us long to be seen and heard. When we're grieving, this becomes even more important.

Your coworker saw you. They listened. They heard not only your words, but your heart. They didn't evaluate you or attempt to fix you. You were able to share and to grieve, freely and safely. No wonder you felt better.

You're right. You need to talk. You need to share what you're thinking and feeling. You need to talk about your child.

Thank God for His provision. He puts the people around us that we need. He expresses His goodness and His love through them. He is at work for us, for you, all the time.

I rejoice with you. Safe people are a true gift from God.

Now that you have purified yourselves by obeying the truth so that you have sincere love for each other, love one another deeply, from the heart.
1 Peter 1:22

Lord, put people in my life who are safe and loving. Lead me to them. You know my needs. Help me to trust You.

61

*Being listened to and heard felt so good,
I decided to return the favor.*

*I contacted a friend whom I knew might
be struggling. I let them talk.*

*Before we ended the call, they told me how much
the conversation had meant to them.*

*All I did was listen. Listening is powerful. I
wish I had done more of it in the past.*

I resolve to be a better listener in the future.

*I was able to give something. I believe I
made a difference. That felt good.*

I could almost see my child smiling.

*If I can serve others while enduring this terrible
loss, perhaps that will help me heal.*

Listening is powerful indeed.

Our world is noisy. Everyone seems busy beyond belief. We race frantically through our days, checking off items on our mental to-do lists. We rarely take time to listen. We all end up missing out.

We all have hearts. We've all been wounded. We all need relationships. We all need to be heard.

Listening is one of life's greatest skills.

The Lord is always listening. He knows you and hears your heart. He is the ultimate listener. When we listen, we reflect Him.

When we feel heard, we heal a little. No wonder it felt good.

Listening well and without judgment is one way you can honor your child and love those around you. When you meet people where they are, as they are, you are doing to others as you would have them do to you.

This is the way of love and blessing in this current grief wilderness. Journey with God today.

My dear brothers and sisters, take note of this: Everyone should be quick to listen, slow to speak and slow to become angry...
James 1:19

Lord, give me a listening heart. Let me hear Your voice. Let me hear the hearts of others. Work in and through me.

62

Work continues to be a challenge.

I've fallen into a rhythm of steeling myself to be fake, survive the day, and grieve in little bits here and there when I can.

Honestly, work is a welcome distraction at times. It gives my mind somewhere to go.

I wish I could focus more. I still blip out at times.

I try not to think about the next grief burst—when, where, what I'm going to do, etc. I can easily walk around cringing, waiting for the ceiling to fall. I refuse to do that. I don't want to live that way.

My heart isn't in my work. I'm just going through the motions. The emptiness inside me feels massive.

I wish things were different.

I wish I had my child back.

Much of your heart is taken up with grief at present. The loss of your child is taking up enormous space. There's less of you available for work. Because your life has changed, your work is different too.

Distractions can be healthy. Our hearts can't handle the intensity of our grief 24-7. Zoning out is natural and even healthy. Your heart and mind are taking a much-needed break.

Grief bursts will come but focusing on them only leads to anxiety and fear. God is with you. He can handle it. You will get through it.

Grief bursts are essentially pressure releases for your heart. You're expressing love for your child. You're feeling their absence.

Your work performance won't be at the usual level right now—and that's okay. You're missing your child. Give yourself a lot of mercy and grace.

God is at work in and through you. Accept yourself. Receive His love for you. Look for His gifts today.

I pray that out of His glorious riches he may strengthen you with power through His Spirit in your inner being, so that Christ may dwell in your hearts through faith.
Ephesians 3:16-17

God, You can handle all things. I release myself and all things to You. Strengthen me.

63

Yes, I can see that I need people who know grief. I need other grieving parents.

I need someone who gets it. I need someone who's been through something similar who can empathize and relate.

Where do I find these people? Do I look online? What do I search for?

I don't know about a group. Trusting people I don't know when I'm this vulnerable is unnerving. But I know support groups exist for people like me, right?

When I imagine being with someone who understands, my heart begins to relax. Perhaps looking for a group would be good for me.

I feel like I need a safety net. Perhaps other people—people who understand—can provide some of that safety and support.

God created us in His image. He created us for a relationship with Himself and for relationships with others. We desperately need good, safe connections, especially when we're grieving. Especially when we've lost a child.

Yes, you need others who get it. You need other grieving parents.

Others who have lost children can be a blessing in our lives beyond description. These bereaved moms and dads are traveling the same road. They're facing many of the same challenges and obstacles.

We need people who will let us mention our child's name and talk about them. Other grieving parents understand this need. Their compassion and empathy come from personal experience.

Sometimes bereaved parents find each other by "accident"—at work, at church, in our neighborhood, or even at the grocery store. Many times, we can sense the connection right away. Instant bonds of understanding can occur.

Grieving moms and dads also find each other in support groups. Just getting together can be helpful, comforting, and healing.

We want to grieve in healthy ways that bring honor to the Lord and our child and also empower us to love those around us. Other grieving parents can help.

Again, God knows who and what you need. He brings people together. Seek Him about this. Release your cares and concerns to Him. Listen to Him in His word. He will speak through what He has already spoken. He will guide you.

Dear friends, let us love one another, for love comes from God. Everyone who loves has been born of God and knows God. Whoever does not love does not know God, because God is love.
1 John 4:7-8

Lord, connect me with other grieving parents. Guide me in steps I need to take in this. I present myself to You. Fulfill Your plans and purposes for me.

64

I'm feeling guilty again.

Actually, I probably feel guilty on some level all the time.

I find myself thinking about what I could have done or should have said. I ruminate over the mistakes I made. It seems like every parenting misstep I ever thought I made is staring me in the face.

I know I'm not perfect, but I wish I could have been a better parent. More loving. More patient. More everything.

Then I have the terrible thought I can't seem to shake. I keep wondering if I caused this somehow. Am I responsible?

Sometimes I think, "Yes, it's my fault."

That's devastating. I can't stay there long, or I end up in a very dark place.

The guilt is stifling. Sometimes I can barely breathe.

Guilt is like a boomerang. It keeps coming back. It circles back around, over and over again.

When we lose a child, it's natural to look back and remember. When we do, we see regrets as well as joys. Regrets often morph into guilt.

Regret says, "I wish I had done things differently. I wish I had done this-or-that. If I had known then what I know now, I would have..."

Guilt says, "It's my fault. I caused this. I'm responsible."

Regrets must simply be accepted as such over time. We don't hold ourselves hostage over them.

Guilt, however, is poison to the heart.

The antidote for guilt is forgiveness. Jesus died for all our sins – past, present, and future. Receiving His forgiveness sets us free from guilt's persistent accusations.

Share your regrets with the Lord. Present your heart and anything you feel guilty about to Him. Lay your "what-if's" and "if-only's" before Him. Watch His face. See His love and acceptance. Embrace His total forgiveness.

Whenever guilt comes knocking, accept God's forgiveness and accept yourself. Release the guilt. Let it pass on through.

If you, Lord, kept a record of sins, Lord, who could stand? But with You there is forgiveness, so that we can, with reverence, serve You.
Psalm 130:3-4

Lord, here is my heart. Your forgiveness is perfect. I rest in what Christ did for me. I receive Your acceptance and love.

65

How in the world do I parent my other kids right now?

What are they feeling? What thoughts are going through their minds? What are they struggling with?

Sometimes they seem fine. Other times they seem different.

At times, they are not themselves—at least, not who they used to be.

I can hardly think about this. My own grief is over the top and all-consuming. I don't have space for any extra challenges.

I don't know how to manage this.

I feel like a failure.

When a child dies, grief naturally begins to invade and even take over our lives. We're shocked, stunned, and often paralyzed.

Our normal routine is gone. Our old life is gone. Everything has changed. No wonder we struggle with parenting our other children during this time.

The death of one child throws everything into a tailspin for a time. Parenting was difficult before. Now it can seem next to impossible.

We don't know what to do for ourselves. How could we know what to do for our other children?

Some parents have no kids left. The child who died was their only child—or perhaps their only child left. This brings a different set of grief challenges.

As bereaved parents, we're all in uncharted territory. We've never been here before, even if we've lost other children. All the terrain around us is new and often dark and foreboding.

As followers of Jesus Christ, we acknowledge that our children are gifts from God and personally created by Him. As the ultimate Father, God knows the pain of being separated from those He created and loves.

As grieving moms and dads, we look to God for the strength and capacity to embrace this grief and pain. In our weakness and exhaustion, we cry out to our Father for our other kids. And we keep crying out to Him.

Our Savior Jesus tells us not to worry about tomorrow. Today, He says, has enough trouble of its own. Look to Him. Let the grief come. Release worry and fear. Give yourself and your children to Him.

But seek first His kingdom and His righteousness, and all these things will be given to you as well. Therefore do not worry about tomorrow, for tomorrow will worry about itself. Each day has enough trouble of its own.
Matthew 6:33-34

Lord, I give myself to You. I give my other kids to You. You gave us to each other. I'm brokenhearted and overwhelmed. I release all things to You.

66

I don't know what to do to help myself. I don't know what to do to help my spouse. And I certainly don't know what to do for my other kids.

I try to be strong for them. I find myself hiding my grief and trying to present stability and normalcy. I don't think I'm succeeding.

Keeping my grief inside and being strong for others is taking its toll on me. I can almost feel my insides being slowly ground into little pieces. It's like I'm losing more of myself and my family every day.

God would want me to be strong, right?

God doesn't give us more than we can handle, right?

If I'm living by faith, I should be able to plow through this victoriously, right?

Right?

I guess it all depends on what it means to be strong.

According to the Bible, we have no strength in ourselves. All of our strength comes from God. He is our strength.

Jesus told us, "Apart from Me, you can do nothing."

The Apostle Paul, writing about some of the troubles he faced, said, "We were under great pressure, far beyond our ability to endure, so that we despaired of life itself."

I don't know about you, but this world routinely gives me

more than I can handle. It's not about me handling life. It's about me following Jesus and doing life with Him amid all the challenges.

Paul also wrote, "And He said to me, 'My grace is sufficient for you, for My power is made perfect in weakness.' Therefore, I will boast about my weaknesses so that Christ's power may rest on me.'"

Perhaps instead of trying to be strong, we need to embrace our weakness. We control nothing. We are completely dependent on God for all and everything. He is our strength.

The Apostle Paul told us, "I can do all things through Christ who strengthens me" (or through Christ, who is my strength).

I am weak. God is all-powerful. I have no strength apart from Him. I can do nothing apart from Jesus. As I continually give myself to Jesus, He works in and through me.

As bereaved parents, this is way beyond our abilities and individual strength. Cling to Jesus. Lean hard into your heavenly Father. Pour out your heart to Him. Rest. Receive. Let Him be strong for you.

I know what it is to be in need, and I know what it is to have plenty. I have learned the secret of being content in any and every situation, whether well fed or hungry, whether living in plenty or in want. I can do all this through Him who gives me strength.
Philippians 4:12-13

Lord, I confess that I am weak. I can't handle this. You can. I'll fix my eyes on You. Empower me to walk with You today step by step.

67

What do I do with my child's things?

*I've been putting off even asking that question.
I don't want to deal with this.*

*At first, I thought I would keep everything forever.
Then I thought I might give everything away.*

Now, I don't know.

I can't leave things as they are, can I? Reminders of my child are everywhere. Every possession seems packed with memories. Right now, most of those memories bring pain.

Will it always be this way?

I know dealing with my child's things is part of this whole process, but I don't know what I should do or how.

Dealing with a child's belongings is a difficult, painful part of the grief process. There is no right way or perfect timing to do this. Every bereaved parent's grief journey is unique.

Some deal with their child's possessions quickly, while others take years. Most parents tackle this challenge in stages, deciding over time what they want to keep and what they want to give away.

Our child's belongings are special because they are what we have left. They represent our child to us, and our hearts are reluctant to say goodbye and let go.

The Lord feels your pain and knows your heart. Ask Him for guidance. What would be most loving toward Him, yourself, and your child?

Take your time. Let your heart be guided by love.

Peter went with them, and when he arrived, he was taken upstairs to the room. All the widows stood around him, crying and showing him the robes and other clothing that Dorcas had made while she was still with them.
Acts 9:39

Lord, reminders of my child are everywhere. I don't know what to do, how, or when. Guide me. I will rest in You and trust that You will lead me.

68

I decided to go through my child's things a little bit at a time.

Surprisingly, some items are easy to deal with. Other things, however, I put right back in the drawer or box. I guess I'm not ready to decide about those yet.

I'm amazed how things can carry a person's presence. Most of my child's possessions have memories attached to them. My emotions surge up and bounce all over the place. This is hard.

I tell myself it's just a bunch of stuff, but my heart isn't getting the message. This is going to take a lot of time and energy. I guess I need to either push through or adjust my expectations.

Pushing through doesn't seem right or healthy at this point.

Breathe. I need to breathe.

After the death of a child, we naturally cling tightly to what we have left. Possessions are attached to people. Some things become infinitely precious after a loss.

For most bereaved parents, dealing with their child's possessions is an emotional roller coaster. Drawers, closets, boxes, and rooms are stuffed with potential grief triggers. We see something, and the memories come flooding in. We touch something else, and our hearts mourn.

Thankfully, the same basic grief truths apply to possessions. God is with you and in you. Be real with Him and share what's happening inside you. Be patient and loving toward yourself. Take your time.

The goal is not to deal with your child's possessions. The goal is intimacy with God amid the pain and confusion.

Grief is not a checklist, but a journey of the heart. One moment, one step at a time.

***Because You are my help, I sing in the
shadow of Your wings. I cling to You;
Your right hand upholds me.
Psalm 63:7-8***

*I cling to You, Lord. This broken walk is about
intimacy with You. I will focus on You and trust
that You will make all things clear in time.*

69

My emotions are stirred up from dealing with my child's possessions—or trying to. I feel agitated, sad, and lost.

My grief feels extra heavy at present. I feel like I'm going backwards.

I seem to be reliving so much. Memories swirl around me. I feel dizzy sometimes.

The more emotional I am, the more challenging work and relationships become. Grief makes everything harder.

When I'm more of a mess, I want to withdraw. I pull back and start protecting myself more. I've had enough pain.

I've been at this grief thing for a while now, but I still feel lost and alone. I feel overwhelmed and shaky right now.

Will this ever get any better? Do I really want it to get better?

Sometimes I think I want to stay right here, immersed in this heavy grief.

I miss my child. I long to see their face and hear their voice.

Grief is always moving. Like any journey, some portions will be harder and more demanding than others.

On this bereaved parent walk, so much is painful, sad, and frustrating. Some parts of your grief path will be especially rocky, uphill, and challenging. You can only take one step at a time and live one moment at a time. The task is learning to navigate what's in front of you in a sane and healthy way, while trying not to jump ahead.

As you process your grief, it will change over time.

Grief is unpredictable, and we never know what's coming next. But we do know God. He is constant. He never changes. He is forever the same. He is love.

As much as possible, be authentic with Him. Share honestly with Him about what's happening inside you. Yes, He already knows, but He wants to hear it from you. He loves to listen to the voice of your heart.

***Jesus Christ is the same yesterday
and today and forever.
Hebrews 13:8***

Everything seems to be changing. You, Lord, never change. I rest in You. You are my constant, faithful companion on this rocky road of grief.

70

I don't feel like me anymore. And it's getting worse.

I long for my child. I miss them desperately.

I miss my old life. I miss my family as it used to be.

I miss me.

I find myself wondering who I am now.

I wonder if I'm going to make it through this. If I do, I wonder what I'll be like on the other side of this grief.

I'm wondering about a lot right now. I'm in some in-between place that seems uncertain and foggy.

I feel like I'm drifting, but don't know where.

The loss of a child tends to throw most parents into a sort of identity crisis. Since we're designed by God for relationship, the death of a child can deal a stunning blow to our sense of who we are.

In an instant, with our child's final breath, we find ourselves in another world. Our life has been altered. Everything takes on a different hue and shade. This loss hits the heart, and therefore affects everything.

We find ourselves in the valley of the shadow of death that King David talks about in Psalm 23. We're no longer in green pastures or beside still waters. We're in an unfamiliar and foreboding place. It can feel dark and scary.

Psalm 23 reminds us that journeying through such places is part of this life. But it is also a valley that we emerge from. It might be hard to grasp, but the implication is that there is more green grass on the other side of this season of grief.

God is leading you through this territory. Through is the key word. Now is not forever.

Be kind to yourself. Rest in God's kindness, goodness, and love. He will guide you. Lean into Him today.

Even though I walk through the darkest valley,
I will fear no evil, for You are with me; Your
rod and Your staff, they comfort me.
Psalm 23:4

You walk with me, Lord. You lead me. You
are my constant companion. I am Yours. I will
trust You and take one step at a time.

71

I know there is good all around me. I can see it. In my family. In people. In life.

At the same time, I can't seem to feel the good that's there. I'm surrounded with love, but I can't embrace it.

Lately, I feel nothing. My child is no longer here.

My heart is crushed. My emotions have exhausted me.

I don't think I have any feelings left.

I'm empty. Tired.

And then I think of all my responsibilities. I want to hide.

You're grappling with the death of your precious child. Your heart is exhausted with grief. Your heart is taking a break, trying to recover. No wonder you feel numb.

Yes, there is good all around you. You will appreciate and feel the good again, but perhaps not right now.

This is frustrating. We can feel disconnected and not part of the world around us. We're dazed. We're exhausted and numb.

I think of the final verse in Psalm 23. This was King David's summation of life. "Surely goodness and love will follow me all the days of my life, and I will dwell in the house of the Lord forever."

We need not chase love and goodness. Love and goodness are

all around us. God surrounds us with them. Goodness and love accompany and follow us wherever we go. God, who is love, is with us and in us. He is goodness.

Jesus is with you. He walks with you. He knows all about grief, pain, and suffering. Breathe. Rest in Him.

You may not feel like you're experiencing any goodness right now. That's okay. As a bereaved parent, it's hard to feel much of anything sometimes.

I remain confident of this: I will see the goodness of the Lord in the land of the living. Wait for the Lord; be strong and take heart and wait for the Lord.
Psalm 27:13-14

Though many times I don't feel it, I trust that I am surrounded by your love and goodness, Lord. Give me eyes to see You. Let me experience your love.

72

I used to wake up in the morning and look forward to the day. I expected good things. I had joy.

Now I open my eyes and lie there, deeply aware of my child's absence.

I force myself to get moving. Everything seems to take much more mental energy. I feel depressed.

I'm sluggish. It's like I'm not all here. It's as if I have half a heart. Part of me is missing.

My motivation is waning. My sense of purpose has almost disappeared.

My child is gone. I feel undone.

I feel like a shadow.

Grief can take its toll over time. The heaviness of this unthinkable loss naturally weighs us down. Routine life takes much more conscious effort and energy.

Since we're created by God for relationship, when a child (no matter what age) dies, our hearts are shaken, broken, and even shattered.

At first, we're stunned. As life continues, we feel the pain. We keep trying to hobble along, but sometimes wonder if we're going anywhere.

Your child is missing from all the spaces in your life they used to occupy. Your world has been vastly altered. You feel this intensely. Your heart knows. Life is different. You are different.

The Lord is your strength, your energy, your life. He holds your heart. He heals you bit by bit as you are real with Him about what's happening inside you. Keep releasing all things to Him. He will never leave you or forsake you.

This is a season of deep grief, and the Lord is guiding you through it. He is good. He is faithful. He is love.

You, Lord, keep my lamp burning; my
God turns my darkness into light.
Psalm 18:28

Lord, I have no strength apart from You. My heart is broken. Be merciful to me and heal me. You are my light and my hope.

73

*Will things ever feel good again? Will I have
joy again? Is it okay to have joy?*

*I feel like I should be sad, but I don't like it.
When I do smile, I feel guilty later.*

*My mind is saying it's wrong to have anything good right now. It's
as if joy would be disrespectful and wrong. I feel caught. Stuck.*

*I don't know if I'm the one making decisions
right now, or if grief is driving me along.*

I don't feel in charge of my life, my emotions, or anything.

*I'm at the whim of events, other people's words and
reactions, and my own unpredictable emotions.*

*I'm in this dark, gloomy room called parental
grief and I can't seem to get out.*

God is gracious. He gives relief amid pain. He gives joy and delight to grieving hearts. He shines light in dark places. All this is true, even though you may not feel it at present.

Your child would not deny you joy. They would not wish guilt and pain upon you. If they could, they would shower you with peace, healing, and contentment.

Now is a season of grief, but it is not a time bereft of hope and joy. Hope and joy are always here, but perhaps you don't feel them the way you're used to. You may not be able to feel them right now.

It can feel like you're being swept along by a river of grief, trapped in its strong, swift current. In reality, you're on an unknown path, walking with the Lord, taking one step at a time. The Lord knows this path, though you do not.

Your grief honors your child. Take your emotions seriously. Feel them. Be honest with God about them today. He is your light. He is with you in your darkest places. He embraces your grieving heart.

Very truly I tell you, you will weep and mourn while the world rejoices. You will grieve, but your grief will turn to joy.
John 16:20

Lord, I accept this season of grief. Now is not forever. I will receive and treasure the joy You give me along the way. You are my light.

74

I feel limp and lifeless.

No stamina. No motivation. No sense of purpose or direction.

I'm just here, going through the motions. All my energy is focused on getting through the day, somehow, some way.

I don't know how long I can do this. I need something to change.

I don't like this new life. It's like my heart has departed. Perhaps my heart is gone.

Maybe it left with my child.

I loved my child desperately. I love them still. I never dreamed I would have to do life without them. I still feel like their parent.

I don't know how to do this. I know life goes on. I know God is with me. I know all these things, but this still hurts.

I feel so lost and alone.

In the intense grief from the loss of a child, the heart mourns at depths we didn't know were possible. The agony of it all is overwhelming. We don't know how to process this. We don't know what to think or how to feel.

Life becomes not only painful, but confusing. All our energies become focused on the essentials of life: moving, working, eating, sleeping, and fulfilling responsibilities. These routine things now require Herculean effort. There is little to no energy left for anything else.

Our sense of purpose takes a hit. With our child gone, we can wonder why we're here. Who are we now? Our motivation seems to evaporate.

God carries us all the time. We never walk, work, or do life on our own. In seasons of grief, we become even more conscious of this. Our fragility and vulnerability come to the surface, and we don't like it.

God carries you. He is your life. You were made for a relationship with Him. He walks with you. The Lord knows your wounds. He is your Healer.

When He rose from prayer and went back to the disciples, He found them asleep, exhausted from sorrow.
Luke 22:45

Lord, grief has exhausted me. You are my hope, my strength, and my life. Heal my wounds. I rest in You. I trust You.

75

I know I've said this before. I don't feel like me anymore.

I miss my child. I miss our relationship. I miss our family as it used to be. I miss my old life. I miss everything.

I don't know how to navigate this new and unpredictable terrain. I don't know who I am. I don't know why I'm here. I seem to have lost my sense of identity and purpose.

What do I do?

Do I keep getting up in the morning, hoping that my heart and sense of purpose will return someday?

Life seems so dull and gray. My sunshine is gone. Everything seems gloomy.

When the sun does peek through, it's almost as if I chase it away. It's like I don't want to be happy. I can't.

Grieving parents wonder about many things.

Everything can seem uncertain and up in the air. We can feel lost. It's as if a sinkhole opened under us and we're in a free fall to who knows where.

Fear of the unknown can threaten our hearts. We brace for more loss. Our sense of hope diminishes.

Your world has been altered. Without your child, nothing

is quite the same. Your heart has been broken. This affects everything.

Even with all this, your purpose is still there, safe and intact. As you walk with the Lord through this valley, He will speak to you. He is your comfort. He is your strength. He is your purpose.

No matter what you might feel at any given moment, God has not distanced Himself or disappeared. He's in this with you, all the way.

Right now, you're in grief recovery. This takes time and loads of energy. God is working in you and through you more than you realize. He is giving to you, even in this season when you feel so empty.

You may not feel these realities. That's okay. Accept yourself. Lean into God. Keep your heart open to Him. Share openly and honestly. He is listening. He knows your heart.

Look to the Lord and His strength;
seek His face always.
Psalm 105:4

My world is upended. Lord, I look to You. You are my strength. You know all things. Amid the turmoil, I choose to seek You.

76

*I now understand a little more why people
run to alcohol, drugs, or food.*

*The pain of life can be immense. The fear and worry can
drive a person to the brink. The emptiness inside feels huge.*

*I want relief. I've noticed I'm drinking more. It
used to be a glass of wine here and there. Now, it's
more than a glass, more than occasionally.*

*I don't think I'm an alcoholic, at least not yet. I'm
trying to get through this time as sanely as possible. If
I'm drinking more, does that mean I'm depressed?*

I'm caring less and less about things, about myself, and about life.

*I never dreamed this could happen, but it did. I never
stop feeling the loss. I will never stop missing my child.*

None of us like pain, especially emotional pain. We don't know what to do with it. We tend to run from it rather than feeling it through. The emotional pain of losing a child is indescribable.

At times, we hunger for relief. We run to food, alcohol, work, shopping, hobbies, entertainment, and drugs. If something promises relief and distraction, we lunge for it.

Of course, none of these things satisfy. As grief relief, they don't work. The grief is still there, and the emotional pain boomerangs back with a vengeance. Now we have extra guilt to deal with too.

As we are honest with ourselves, the Lord, and a few other people about what's going on inside us, some of this internal pressure is released. We feel some of the pain and process some of the grief. The need for addictions wanes.

Breathe. See the Lord walking with you in this pain. He longs for you to give yourself to Him so that He can work in and through you and bring comfort, peace, and hope.

The Lord feels your pain. Lay your heart in His hands. Experience His love today.

And I pray that you, being rooted and established in love, may have power, together with all the Lord's holy people, to grasp how wide and long and high and deep is the love of Christ, and to know this love that surpasses knowledge—that you may be filled to the measure of all the fullness of God.
Ephesians 3:17-19

Lord, enable me to experience Your perfect love. Surround me with it and immerse me in it. Calm my troubled, shattered heart. You are love. You are life.

77

I know I need safe, trustworthy people in my life right now. I'm having trouble finding them.

People that I counted on are gone, or at least most of them. Disappeared. Poof. It's like losing a child is a disease, and I'm contagious.

People are avoiding me. I can sense it.

I'm angry. Then I laugh. If I were them, I would avoid me too. Who wants to be around this kind of sorrow and pain?

I feel alone in the world, even if I'm surrounded by other people. My agony is so deep that no one else can possibly relate. At least, that's the way it feels.

I feel more isolated by the day. I can look back and see myself pulling away.

I know this isn't healthy, but my pain and disappointment with how other people respond seems to be driving me more and more inside myself.

I don't know what to do. I need help.

When we don't know what to do, we back up to what we know to be true, no matter what.

What is true?

God is real. He thought of you, wanted you, and planned you

even before He created the earth and the world. He loved you, and He loves you still. His love is perfect. He created you for relationship with Himself and others. He places people in your life, and you in theirs.

We're designed to love each other and do life together. He has safe people out there for you.

Safe people meet you where you are in your grief. They accept you as you are. They listen well. They don't try to fix or help you feel better. They are content to love you by walking with you in your pain.

No one is perfect. Even safe people mess up from time to time. Overall, however, they can be trusted with your heart.

You need some people that know grief and know it well. Some grieving parents find these people in support groups. People who were on the periphery of your life, or perhaps some you didn't know at all, can become major players in your recovery, healing, and growth.

Safe people who know grief will gladly walk with you through this painful, uncharted territory—especially others who have experienced the loss of a child. Ask God to bring these people into your life. Ask Him to guide you to them.

Perhaps you know who they are already. Reach out. Your heart needs support. You're more important than you realize.

But if we walk in the light, as He is in the light, we have fellowship with one another, and the blood of Jesus, His Son, purifies us from all sin.
1 John 1:7

*Lord, open my eyes to recognize the safe people around me.
I want heart connection. I need fellowship.
Surround me with healing.*

78

What are support groups like anyway?

I don't think of myself as a timid person, but the idea of showing up to a group fills me with fear and dread. I'm already feeling vulnerable and on edge.

Will talking about the loss of my child with other people help? What if they judge me?

Support groups sound a bit scary.

It feels risky.

Part of me says, "No way. I'm going to do this alone. It's safer that way." But then, I know where that kind of thinking leads – to greater loneliness and isolation.

How do I do this? Where do I go?

I'm apprehensive.
Will they take my heart and my pain seriously?

Most grieving parents are reluctant to try a support group. It takes courage and resolve to enter a room of people you don't know when your heart is already shaking.

Healing is a battle. Your heart is under assault. Grief is not the enemy, but guilt, isolation, bitterness, and self-condemnation are. It's a spiritual battle.

We don't fight these enemies alone. We need courageous companions in it with us. There are others out there – and other grieving parents among them – who are ready and able to walk with you through this season of grief.

Is there a grief support group at your church? If not, is there one at a church near you? Perhaps try local hospices. If you can't find a physical group, there are grief support groups available online.

Most of the good and healing things in life are scary and require courage. In this case, it requires faith. Trust is displayed one step at a time. Just take the next step.

God has people out there to walk with you through this. Though it might be hard to imagine, He wants to use you in their lives too.

"Be strong and courageous. Do not be afraid; do not be discouraged, for the Lord your God will be with you wherever you go."

Joshua 1:9

God, You are my strength. Work in me and move me to places and people of hope and healing. You go before me. Give me courage and faith to follow.

79

You said God wants to use me in other people's lives? Honestly, that's hard to imagine. Maybe in the future, but surely not like I am now.

I'm a mess. I'm no good to anyone.

My own family sighs when they see or talk to me. My friends avoid me. Everyone wants me to get over this, as if the death of my child is like the common cold.

I'm focused on survival, and I'm not doing well at even that. Every day is like doing water aerobics in the middle of the ocean. No relief. Just more exhaustion.

I sound terribly cynical, don't I? I wonder where my faith went. I know it's still there, but it must be hiding somewhere. I certainly don't feel it.

I miss my old life. I miss my child.

Grief is taking up huge amounts of space in your life at present. It's demanding and draining. There's less of you left for the rest of life. No wonder you're frustrated.

Even if everyone around you seems to be avoiding you, trying to fix you, and pelting you with platitudes and advice, there are people out there who are supportive. Your loss and grief are unique, but some understand what it means to be hurt, confused, crushed, or even devastated. There are many bereaved parents out there.

These fellow grievers are not only out there, but they're also waiting for you. They're looking for people like you to walk with them.

You don't have to be on the top of your game for God to use you. You just have to be willing. God can use anyone, anytime, anywhere.

You will often be unaware that God is working in and through you. That happens as you trust Him and simply show up.

If trying a support group is still scary, consider asking a friend to go with you the first time. Feeling weak and vulnerable amid this terrible grief is common for bereaved parents.

Be joyful in hope, patient in affliction, faithful in prayer...Rejoice with those who rejoice; mourn with those who mourn.
Romans 12:12, 15

You are always at work and things are not always as they seem to be. I present myself to You. I believe You live in me. Live through me, Lord.

80

*Grief and mourning are exhausting. My brain is
tired. My mind is not what it used to be.*

*I'm forgetting things—more than usual.
I can't seem to think straight.*

*I have trouble finding words when I'm in conversation.
I blink and forget what we were talking about.*

*I thought it was just the fatigue. Now I don't know. I'm
worried there might be something wrong with me.*

*I don't feel like myself at all. It feels like
my brain isn't working right.*

Is this grief too?

I miss my child desperately.

Most likely, yes—it's grief. If you're concerned about your health, however, please get checked out. Sometimes, we need reassurance more than anything.

Grief affects us mentally, especially with the loss of a beloved child. Our cognitive functions aren't what they used to be.

Grief is taking up much of your internal space. Details—like where you put something, appointments, and what you were just talking about—tend to fall through the cognitive cracks.

As you walk with the Lord and move through your grief,

the mental fog will begin to clear over time. Those cognitive abilities you miss will most likely bounce back with proper self-care.

The Lord knows your limitations. Though you may not be aware of it, He is handling many, many things for you, right now. The Lord is patient with you. Be patient with yourself.

God is comforting and ministering to you in your pain and grief. He is healing your heart, though at times you may not feel that way. He is good, and His love for you is perfect.

But David found strength in the Lord his God.
1 Samuel 30:6

Lord, You are patient with me. Enable me to be patient with myself. You are my life. I release all worry and concern to You.

81

I'm still not sleeping well.

I wake up at night. My mind races. I lie there, thinking about my child.

Their absence is palpable. The silence is crushing. Everything descends upon me in the dark. Guilt swirls in my brain.

I often wake up sweating and anxious. I have dreams—and a few nightmares.

I see my child in my mind's eye in the middle of the night. The sadness is intense. The questions start circling again. I feel like I'm right back where I started.

No matter how much time goes by, my child's death seems like yesterday. The feelings are fresh, all over again, for the hundredth time.

Almost all grieving parents report that nighttime is difficult. We lay our heads on the pillow and our minds flow to where our hearts are -- with our departed child.

Our thoughts begin to race, faster and faster. Waking up to an anxiety attack is not uncommon. Our minds and hearts are processing our pain and grief, even while we sleep.

As you lie there at night, breathe deeply. Try to focus on your breathing. See the Lord with you—because He is. Hear Him speaking to you—comforting and reassuring you.

He is always speaking to us. We need ears to hear Him.

Turn your thoughts toward Him. Tune in to His voice. Slow down the thought train and let His word bathe your mind and heart.

God is with you in the night. He is speaking. He is listening. He is loving you, even while you sleep.

If I say, "Surely the darkness will hide me and the light become night around me," even the darkness will not be dark to You; the night will shine like the day, for darkness is as light to You.
Psalm 139:11-12

Lord, You are my constant companion. You never leave me. Speak to me and bring Your comfort in the night. Give me sleep. I rest in You.

82

*I found a support group. I haven't contacted anyone
yet, but I know where and when it meets.*

*I'm still nervous about this. My mind says, "Don't bother. It's
not going to help. This will be a waste of time and energy."*

*Then I think, "Why not go and try it? What do I have to lose?
Yes, this is scary, but I've done plenty of scary things in my life."*

*I wish I knew what it was going to be like. That
would help. I feel like I need to be emotionally
and mentally prepared to walk in there.*

I wish I were less fearful – and more courageous.

*It seems like my courage and confidence
departed with my child.*

Almost every bereaved parent wonders these things about support groups. If there's a contact person or number to call, reach out. Ask them for more information. They'll gladly tell you what the group is like and how it operates. You might even be able to talk to the leader or facilitator. Reaching out takes energy, but it's well worth it.

It's not really about courage, but about faith. Do you believe God will be with you as you go and bless you no matter what? Do you believe He has people there He has prepared for you, and you for them?

As the writer of the book of Hebrews says, "Now faith is confidence in what we hope for and assurance about what we do not see" (11:1).

It can be difficult, in times of loss, to look for and see the good. We can set our minds on God and His goodness, even amid this terrible pain. Our hearts need the reassurance that He is ordering all things for our good. Our minds need the reminder that He has a plan for us—a good plan.

Chew on God's Word. Breathe deeply and take in what He has said. Listen as He speaks to you.

When fearful or worried, let your mind go to comforting, uplifting scriptures. God speaks through what He has spoken.

He is speaking now.

I rise before dawn and cry for help; I have put my hope in Your word. My eyes stay open through the watches of the night, that I may meditate on Your promises.
Psalm 119:147-148

Lord, You are always speaking. Open my ears to hear Your voice. Let me look to You above anyone else or anything else for comfort, courage, and guidance.

83

I'm finding fault with everyone and everything lately. I'm more critical and irritable. I have little to no patience for anyone or anything.

I manage to hold it together in public, but my heart is churning inside. I'm nervous, unsettled, and often angry.

My joy is gone. It departed with my child.

My vision is clouded now. I used to be optimistic. Not anymore. I might smile, but inside I'm all doom and gloom.

I know this isn't helpful, but my mind runs down those dark, hopeless trails anyway. I don't think I like who I'm becoming.

I don't like me. I don't like life. I don't like much of anything right now.

The loss of a child changes everything. This unthinkable death certainly clouds our vision. Loss like this tends to darken our lenses and skew our thinking.

Ultimately, the Lord is the only one who ever sees with total clarity. He knows all, understands all, and is working with all the broken pieces in our lives to build something extraordinary.

God's good work around us and in us is hard to see when our lenses are stained and we're in a pit filled with pain and grief. Our emotions are powerful and can be overwhelming.

Thankfully, God is with us in our pit. He knows every thought and feeling. He reminds us that now is not forever.

He is at work. His arms are around you. Even though you walk in a dark, unfamiliar valley, God your shepherd is leading you to green pastures on the other side. The only way out of this heavy, excruciating grief is through it. Healthy grieving is the way forward.

Your grief honors your child. Your pain is screaming, "I love you."

Lord, be gracious to us; we long for You. Be our strength every morning, our salvation in time of distress.
Isaiah 33:2

You know all things, Lord. You know me. I belong to You. I am Yours. You are with me in this. I trust that You are guiding me, even when I cannot perceive You.

84

I miss my child. I want to see them and be with them so badly.

I never understood how someone could even contemplate taking their own life. Well, now I can see how that's possible.

Pain. Terrible, excruciating, never-ending pain.

I want relief from the pain, from this internal torture. I want a break from the constant cloud of sadness, anger, and longing.

I can see why some would wonder if life is worth it. I can imagine some seeing suicide as a way out. I guess we all have our limits as to what we're willing to endure.

Someone told me I stare and sigh a lot. I'm not surprised. I have a lot to sigh about.

Self-harming thoughts and behaviors are on the rise in our world. Suicide is becoming more acceptable. It's tragic that a forever decision that takes lives is becoming almost a trend.

Life is a gift. All living beings owe their existence to God. He is life and the author of all life. He even came, clothed Himself in human flesh, and died our death on the cross to ensure that life would win.

Our hearts want peace. I'm reminded again of what Jesus said, "I have said these things to you so that in me you may have peace." No one and nothing else can give us peace. When we attempt to replace Him with anyone or anything, our lives shrink and our hearts grow dark.

The loss of a child is traumatic, painful, and confusing. Peace amid the pain and confusion is found in Him. He is peace.

Keep being real and honest with Him. His love for you is limitless. He walks with you today.

Peace I leave with you; my peace I give you. I do not give to you as the world gives. Do not let your hearts be troubled and do not be afraid.
John 14:27

You are my peace. Move me to rest in You. Let me experience Your peace, Lord, more and more with each passing day.

If you're having suicidal thoughts, now or in the future, please involve someone you trust immediately. Call the suicide hotline at 1-800-273-8255, or text "home" to 741741.

85

Well, I went to the support group. I was surprised.

I was terrified beforehand. I found a dozen excuses not to go. But I got in the car, drove there, breathed deeply, and walked in trying to look halfway composed.

I don't know exactly what I expected, but it was different than I had imagined.

They were friendly. Everything was low pressure. Some shared a lot. Some hardly spoke. All of us teared up. Some cried.

I felt better afterwards. I didn't say much, but my heart felt lighter. Perhaps some of my grief pressure got released.

I know these groups aren't always a positive experience. I'm glad my first attempt wasn't a disaster.

I found support in others who are hurting and grieving – people like me.

Every support group is different. Each individual is unique. Though our grief is one-of-a-kind, being with others who are hurting—especially others who have lost children—can be comforting and reassuring.

Fellow grieving hearts remind us that what we're experiencing is common. It's relieving to know we're not crazy. It's okay to not feel okay. Though our loss and grief are unique, connecting with other grievers sends our hearts the message that we're not alone in this.

Of course not all support groups are for everyone. Sometimes you have to try a few to find one that fits well with who and where you are.

God provides who and what we need. Some people might disappear on us, but others will rise to take their place. God is our shepherd. He blesses us with the people we need.

Carry each other's burdens, and in this way you will fulfill the law of Christ.
Galatians 6:2

Lead me, Lord, to supportive people. Let me be safe and supportive for others. Connect me with others who can walk with me in this grief.

86

I feel a little better today. I know that might not mean much, but it feels good.

I know my emotions can change in an instant, but it's nice to have some relief from the constant cloud of oppressive grief.

I'm writing more. I think that might be helping too. My mind moves so fast that I thought getting things down on paper might be good. Writing slows my poor, spinning brain and forces me to focus.

As I write what's going on inside me, I try to release it. I know it may boomerang back.

That's okay. I'll write it down and release it again.

I feel like I'm finally learning how to grieve. I don't like it, but at least I'm not totally hijacked by my emotions all the time.

I miss my child. I love them so much. I still see them everywhere. They are never far from my mind.

Writing can be incredibly cathartic. Whether it's an occasional expression of the heart, consistent journaling, or writing poetry or letters about or to our children, writing can be a wonderful way to process our grief.

You're right about our minds. They spin. Our thoughts ping here and there and then circle back again and again. Writing helps us focus and express what's happening inside. Just getting it out is relieving and beneficial.

David did this frequently in the Psalms. In an intentional and concentrated way, he poured out what he was thinking and feeling. He processed his fear, doubt, emotional pain, and grief.

Writing is one more way we can be honest with ourselves and God.

I wait for the Lord, my whole being waits, and in His word I put my hope. I wait for the Lord more than watchmen wait for the morning...
Psalm 130:5-6

Move me to be honest with You, Lord. Let me hold nothing back. Bring healing to my soul as I walk this path of grief.

87

*What you said about David expressing his heart
and grief to God in the Psalms was helpful. I
knew that, but it hadn't clicked before.*

I decided to tweak how I write. Now, before I begin writing and expressing what I'm feeling and thinking, I write, "To God." In other words, I begin by acknowledging that I'm sharing with Him.

*So far, it's been good. I feel more connected to Him.
I'm sensing His presence more. When I finish writing
an entry, I feel like God and I are in this together. I
know we are, but I haven't felt that way much.*

My heart is still broken. I miss my child desperately.

*I'll keep expressing to God my longings and my loneliness.
Knowing He is with me in this is a huge comfort.*

It sounds like your writing has become prayer.

You're right. God was already with you in this. He knew every thought and emotion, but intentionally including Him and directing it to Him sends a message to your own heart. The message is that God is not only with you, but also that He cares.

God is listening. As you honestly express what's happening inside you to Him, your heart begins to sense His companionship. As you continue this, you will also experience more of His love and peace.

Yes, there will be ups and downs to this. There may be times when He seems a million miles away. Stay the course. Make Him your target and keep expressing your heart. Overall, this will lead to a closer sense of connection with Him. Talk with Him about your child. Share freely with Him.

"To God," is a wonderful way to start anything—writing, drawing, relating, eating, exercising, working, and living. He is your Father. He is the ultimate, perfect parent. He gets it.

And whatever you do, whether in word or deed, do it all in the name of the Lord Jesus, giving thanks to God the Father through Him.
Colossians 3:17

Lord, You are my life. You live in me. I live in You. Make my life about companionship with You. Lead me, my Shepherd. You are my heavenly Father. You are my peace.

88

*The world is a painful mess. So much
death out there. So much tragedy.*

*I know it was there before, but now I seem to be aware of it more.
Loss is everywhere. I see it on the news and in the media. I'm
hearing more about it from neighbors, friends, and coworkers.*

There is more to life than loss, isn't there?

*I feel sad, a little stunned, and perhaps depressed. I look
at the world and don't see colors anymore— only gray.*

*My loss, the death of my child, is one
among millions of other losses.*

*I don't want to be morose. I don't want to be thinking
about death. I want to grieve, but still engage in life. I
want to live well, but right now I'm not sure how.*

*It would be nice to feel joy again, but I
honestly don't know if that's possible.*

When I was a college student, one of my mentors said, "Life is a series of losses."

I nodded. I already knew this to be true.

Then he continued. "How we interpret and respond to those losses makes all the difference."

In other words, how we grieve and live after a loss matters

deeply. I have certainly found this to be accurate in my own experience.

We live in a broken world full of wounded people. We experience loss after loss. If we don't find ways to trust God, grieve in healthy ways, and use these losses for good, the hits of life will end up defining us. We can't afford to let that happen.

You've lost your child – a huge, unthinkable, painful, and confusing loss. You're immersed in a season of grief. While in this season, you'll be especially sensitive to the loss and pain you sense around you. This is natural and common.

Breathe deeply and keep expressing your heart openly to the Lord. Process everything with Him. Though it might be impossible to imagine, the color will return to life one day. Life will never be the same, but it can still be good.

Because of the Lord's great love, we are not consumed, for His compassions never fail.
Lamentations 3:22

Open my eyes and let me see things more from Your perspective, Lord. I give You my pain and grief. Lead me through this lonely wilderness. Comfort my heart.

89

*The next support group meeting is today.
I'm feeling nervous already.*

*I hadn't anticipated this. My first meeting was good,
and I thought I would be looking forward to the next
one. Instead, I find myself wanting to hide.*

*I'm not going to hide, however. I know now that almost
everything healthy in this exhausting process of losing a child
requires courage. Every step forward seems to be scary.*

*I will breathe deeply and go. I'm resolved to do
what's loving for myself and those around me.*

*The facilitator recommended coming at least three
times because each meeting is somewhat different, and
some are better than others. That makes sense.*

*I may struggle throughout the day. That's okay.
I'm going. I've made that decision.*

*I will trust God with getting me there and with how it
goes tonight. I'm not in charge. I never have been.*

Breathe. Trust. Move.

The struggle you're describing is common. Most grieving parents get nervous when heading to support groups—or perhaps gatherings of any kind. Bereaved moms and dads can often feel their hearts shaking with grief—grief that needs to be expressed.

The grief is trying to find its way out, and it begins to exert more pressure. This is natural.

You're right. Every step forward in healthy grieving takes courage. Another way to think of it is that healthy grieving requires us to exercise faith. We're not in control. We're completely dependent on God for life itself and all else. That can be scary.

Being healthy demands that we embrace reality—as God enables us. He is good. He is perfect. Trusting Him is the way to healing, recovery, and peace.

He Himself is our peace and joy. Growth and healing happen as we trust Him, one day, one moment, one step at a time.

The Lord is my strength and my shield; my heart trusts in Him, and He helps me. My heart leaps for joy, and with my song I praise Him.
Psalm 28:7

God, help me to trust You. You are good. Your love endures forever. You are my life, my peace, and my joy. I cling to You.

90

The support group was good. I'm glad I went.

It was hard at times. I emoted more this time than last.

The relieving thing was that I didn't feel embarrassed. Instead, I felt safe and free. Free to grieve. I haven't felt that until now. It felt good. It felt right.

I wish there was another meeting tonight. I would be there.

I'm learning. I need other people who "get it." I need other parents in my life who have lost children and know this terrible grief. Safe people. Trustworthy and compassionate people.

Now that I've tasted some of the goodness of having my heart and grief respected, I want more. Much more.

I believe God brings the people we need when we need them. For us, it's never soon enough, but He has His timing for all things.

So much of life—and grief—has to do with timing. We don't know when our hearts are ready for something, but God does.

He has a plan for you, and it's a good plan. He is working in all things to express His love and care for you. He has brought you into a circle of other caring, grieving hearts. And they have embraced you.

As we share our hearts authentically with others and are met with love and acceptance, we tend to feel loved and accepted by God as well.

We're designed to reflect God's loving, comforting, and encouraging nature, but the world entices us away from this. We get caught in demanding routines. We find ourselves surrounded by messages that cause us to construct our own little fortresses. We build walls to protect ourselves.

When we experience love and compassion from others, our walls come down a little. We experience God's goodness through other people, and we want more. Much more.

"By this everyone will know that you are my disciples, if you love one another."
John 13:35

Lord, bring safe and loving people into my life. Make me a safe and loving person. Construct healing relationships all around me. Thank You for Your goodness to me.

91

I find myself wanting to give.

After being in the support group and hearing others' stories – especially from other grieving parents—my compassion is aroused.

I'm not alone. I'm not crazy either. I'm grieving. And I have reason to grieve. But I don't have to stop living.

I'm starting to understand that grieving is living.

My job right now, above all my other responsibilities, is to take care of myself by grieving in the healthiest way possible.

I feel selfish saying that. It sounds so self-focused. Yet, as I care for myself better, I can feel my heart responding. I want to reach out more.

Being with others who know deep grief can have a profound impact on us. God designed us for relationship. He often uses other people to express His care and concern for us.

It sounds like He is doing that for you through this support group. I rejoice with you.

You're not alone. You're not crazy. You're missing someone incredibly special – your child. You're grieving. And right now, grieving well and experiencing God in the process is your heart's priority.

We can't give away what we don't have. As we care for and love ourselves well, it expands our capacity to love and serve others. Good self-care is honoring to God. He created you unique—one-of-a-kind in human history. You embrace this truth when you care for yourself well.

As you begin to treat yourself as God does—with compassion, kindness, mercy, forgiveness, and love—your heart will heal and your desire to give and serve will grow.

"'Love the Lord your God with all your heart and with all your soul and with all your strength and with all your mind'; and, 'Love your neighbor as yourself.'"
Luke 10:27

*Lord, You are love. You live in me.
Let me experience Your love more and
more. Love others through me.*

92

I've tended to put myself last. Everyone and sometimes everything else came first.

Spouse. Kids. Work. Home. Then me.

I thought this was godly. I thought this was what I was supposed to do—sacrifice myself on the altar of everyone else. The result has been fatigue, frustration, and now anger.

The terrible loss of my child and the resulting grief have taught me I don't want to live that way anymore.

How can I give and serve if I'm not taking care of myself first? How can I live from my heart when my tank is near empty, and I'm running on fumes almost all the time?

Yet, I feel guilty. Perhaps I need some sort of spiritual detox.

A spiritual detox might indeed be a good idea.

We're taught to serve others and to pursue a lifestyle of love. This kind of life, however, requires that we live in faith and from our hearts.

Solomon said, "Above all else, guard your heart, for it is the spring from which everything else in life flows." The heart is our most prized possession. If we lose it, we lose everything.

When we trusted Jesus as our Savior, He gave us a new heart.

A heart of love, service, and impact. However, we are not superhuman. We exercise this heart God has given us by seeking Him and getting to know Him. Knowing Him better becomes our priority.

Loss—especially the loss of a child—can drive us to deeper dependence on Him. Knowing the pain of this unthinkable loss, eternity can come more into focus than ever before. We can begin to set our minds on things above, on heavenly things.

Life is about Him—about knowing Him. The better you know Him, the more you will heal and grow— and the more He will live through you. It's not about you doing it. It's about Him living in and through you to do what He wants to do when He wants to do it.

Most of us need a spiritual detox from time to time. As you reorient your life around knowing God, everything else tends to fall into place over time.

I will give you a new heart and
put a new spirit in you…
Ezekiel 36:26

God, I want to know You better.
Move me to focus on You.
Let my relationship with You
flow into all my other relationships.
Heal me, Lord.

93

I've been thinking about the spiritual detox concept.

I think I've bought into some lies along the way in my spiritual life. Those lies have driven me along, exhausted me, and left me floundering.

Losing my child has brought some stunning clarity. I find myself questioning what I do and why. Why do I do this or that? What's the motive behind how I'm living?

Over time, I've lost focus. My passion has waned. This deep grief has sucked me dry.

Now that I'm dry, I can see the emptiness of how I was living. I was going through the motions. Scattered. Distracted. Chasing my tail. I was on a never-ending treadmill. I was moving but going nowhere.

The death of my child threw everything into confusion. My personal electricity shut down and threw me off the treadmill. It hurt terribly, but I'm realizing I don't want to climb on that treadmill again.

Our world is demanding. Responsibilities—both legitimate ones and those that we allow others and the world to place upon us—grow and multiply like weeds in a manicured lawn. Over time, activity and busyness hijack our lives.

God's voice speaks from the Psalms, "Be still and know that I am God."

We don't like being still. We live in an age of instant everything. Constant information overload drives us. Noise fills our lives. We hurry everywhere. We're breathless. Our to-do list is never done.

Though hard and painful, this season of deep grief can be a blessed time. You miss your child. You long for them. Underneath that longing is a yearning for God Himself—and for heaven.

God is calling. He wants to heal your heart, day by day, moment by moment.

"Be still and know that I am God; I will be exalted among the nations. I will be exalted in the earth."
Psalm 46:10

Lord, You are my life. I need a spiritual detox. I look to You. You are always speaking. Cause me to listen. I want to live from the new heart You have given me.

94

I guess I thought that life was about activity. Doing things. Producing. Achieving. Being responsible. Doing the right thing.

Yet, when I read the Bible, I sense something different.

> *Life isn't about me doing things, but about
> God living in me and through me.*
>
> *It's not about me trying to please Him,
> but about me trusting Him.*

I feel like I need to stop and analyze everything I thought was true. It's like I knew who God was but didn't know Him very well.

I knew He loved me, but honestly, I was mostly afraid of Him. Fear of doing something wrong kept driving me to do what I felt was right. My heart was out of sync. I was living from my head more than from my heart. I kept God at a distance.

> *I'm sighing a lot again. I miss my child,
> and I don't know what to do.*
>
> *Yet, I sense I'm on the right track.*

Grief tends to chip away at what we think we believe. What we truly believe comes out in the way we live.

The death of a beloved child naturally brings a lot of things into question. Our hearts tremble. Our souls can be shaken.

This can be a good shaking. If we're willing, this deep grief can lead us back to the Source—God Himself. Though we're in a mental fog, some things become clearer. We're not the same people we were.

We don't want to live like we did. Death has brought perspective. It can fuel in us a desire to live from our hearts in constant companionship with God. This is what we were designed for, but it often takes a tragedy or loss to get our attention.

This life and this world are not all there is. Thank goodness. We can live with eternity in mind. We can live from our hearts.

God is with you. You are part of His story. He is your life.

Jesus answered, "I am the way and the truth and the life. No one comes to the Father except through me."
John 14:6

God, I want to know You better. I want You to be the driving force behind my life and everything I do. Heal me and live through me, Lord.

95

*I have discovered a big lie I was living. I thought I
was what I did. My accomplishments. Achievements.
My family and what I did for them.*

*I was caught in all my roles. Spouse, parent, coworker, employee,
church member, friend, etc. I was running and moving fast.*

What was I afraid of?

Deep down, maybe I was afraid of everything.

*Now, I'm listening to my heart. Life is about God.
Everything else changes and eventually disappears.*

*I believe God gave me a new heart. I believe Jesus lives
inside me. I sense He wants to live through me. Life isn't
about me or about anyone else. It's about Him.*

*I still don't know what to do with this terrible loss. It's like I'm
waking up for the first time in a new world. I miss my child
desperately, but I sense God is healing me,
a little bit at a time.*

You're right. You're not what you do. You are so much more.

You were thought of, wanted, and planned by God. Jesus Christ came and gave His life for you. He conquered death so that He could give His life to you and live His life in you. The universe is about Him. He designed and created it—and you.

Life is about Him. He is life. He is eternal life.

He invites us to change the focus of our thinking from earthly things to Him. It's only in companionship with Him that we begin to understand who we are, what life is about, and why we're here. He brings perspective to things like death, loss, and grief.

If you've trusted in Christ to give you His life and invited Him to live in you, He has become your life. He is the ultimate grief expert. He walks with you. He is in you. You are in Him.

Even amid all the pain for this terrible loss, His love for you never changes. Rest. Be still. Know that He is God.

We know also that the Son of God has come and has given us understanding, so that we may know Him who is true. And we are in Him who is true by being in His Son Jesus Christ. He is the true God and eternal life.
1 John 5:20

Lord, knowing You is everything. I heal as I get to know You better. I heal as I walk with You and receive from You. I heal as You live in and through me.

96

I keep having headaches and stomach issues. These symptoms have gotten worse since my child died.

Some days it's just annoying, but sometimes it's almost debilitating.

I've been to the doctor. They did some blood work and tests. Nothing.

I'm betting it's all grief and stress.

I feel like I go two steps forward and then three steps back. I guess that's how it is during this season of grief.

I'm trying to let go of things that burden me. I'm attempting to grieve in healthy ways, but perhaps I'm failing.

The physical stuff is bad today. I'm discouraged. I felt like I was making progress and taking some leaps forward. Now, I'm not so sure.

The intense grief after the loss of a child is a form of severe stress, and our bodies feel it. The emotional demands are heavy, and our systems get taxed by the constant pressure. It can wear us down after a while.

Our bodies try to keep the stress at bay, but sooner or later we feel our grief physically. Many feel it every day. Headaches, stomach distress, palpitations, exhaustion, aches and pains, and more frequent illnesses are all common.

For some of us, our bodies don't feel the impact until we're processing our grief better. Our brains sense our healthy responses and send the message to our bodies that it's now safe to break down a bit and feel this grief. In other words, more physical distress doesn't necessarily mean you aren't doing well or grieving in healthy ways.

The answer is still the same. Grieve in healthy ways. Care for yourself in this. Let God love you. Rest in Him. He knows every pain and symptom.

Grief is an unpredictable, windy, rock-strewn road. Walk with God. Let Him lead. He is your shepherd.

Listen to my prayer, O God, do not ignore my plea; hear me and answer me. My thoughts trouble me and I am distraught.
Psalm 55:1-2

I feel vulnerable, Lord. I'm easily discouraged. My body is feeling the pressure of life and loss. Enable me to trust You. I release all burdens to You.

97

Life without my child is painful, empty, and lonely.

I try to keep my focus on God. I remind myself that whatever I face today, He can handle it.

I thought I could handle almost anything. Maybe I considered myself invincible, in charge, and in control.

The reality is stunningly different.

I am fragile, but God is with me. I am broken, but God is healing me. I am grieving, but God is walking with me in my pain. I am dependent on Him for all and everything. He is good.

Yes, I know there's a lot of suffering in this world. If He is not good, and if He is not love, then I'm in trouble. We all are.

Lord, have mercy on us.

I think again of Jesus' words, "In this world, you will have trouble." Life is heavy. Loss, demands, and fear come knocking frequently. We are indeed fragile.

We are imperfect. We are flawed and sorely limited. God is our strength. He is our Rock and our Fortress. His love and power are limitless.

You're right that we can't handle this loss or life by ourselves. We weren't meant to.

In God, we can do all things, as He gives us His strength. He lives in and through us. In ourselves, we can't. In Him, we can. He is your resource, your hope, and your life.

The loss of a child is painful and heartbreaking. The Lord knows this. He knows you. He knows your heart. He meets you where you are and walks this lonely road with you.

"I am the vine; you are the branches. If you remain in me and I in you, you will bear much fruit; apart from me you can do nothing."
John 15:5

I am fragile and limited, Lord. You are my strength, my hope, my life. I live in You. You live in me. I will trust You and rest in You today.

98

I can't seem to get on top of things. I'm always spinning.

I used to be a good juggler, but now I have too many balls in the air. My concentration isn't what it was.

I tell myself, "It's okay. I'm grieving. This is common and expected." That helps, but I don't like it.

I find myself wondering if this new life without my child is ever going to get any better.

Will the grief always be this deep and intense? Does the heart ever rebound?

I know I won't be the same and I don't want to be—but I would like to feel better.

Maybe I should just let some balls drop from time to time. I can't keep them all in the air.

Perhaps I'm expecting too much of myself.

We're certainly not the same people after the loss of a child. How could we be?

Our lives are a web of relationships. When one strand—especially a thick, foundational one—is severed, the whole web shakes with the shock. It takes time for the heart to find a new equilibrium. Our world has changed.

As we grieve in healthy ways, we heal and grow. Yet, many of us are surprised by the power and duration of grief.

Wanting to feel better is natural. Grieving is an individual path unique to you, your heart, and your relationship with your child. There are patterns to grief, but no two grief paths are exactly the same.

Therefore, there is no timeline. The grieving process takes as long as it takes. The grief will end when you stop missing your child. That means that, on some level, you'll be grieving the rest of your life. As you heal, however, the grief will change over time.

Walking this grief road is part of trusting God. Keep expressing your heart to Him. He Himself is your peace, your patience, and your endurance.

As you grieve in healthy ways, you will be healing and growing. As much as possible, breathe deeply and walk with God in the present moment.

Lord, my strength and my fortress,
my refuge in time of distress...
Jeremiah 16:19

You, Lord, are my strength, my peace, and my life. I present myself to You today. I am yours. I trust that You are leading, guiding, and healing me.

99

*What can I do for my other kids? How
can I help them with all this?*

*I'm tired of faking it. Yet, I feel strange about grieving
and potentially falling apart in front of them.*

*I feel weird about falling apart anywhere, but I
seem to be a nanosecond away from a meltdown
no matter where I am or what I'm doing.*

*Something tells me that we should be grieving
together somehow. How do we do that?*

*The weight of responsibility is crushing me. I'm just
surviving. Getting through each day requires all I've got. I
feel like I'm doing the bare minimum with everything.*

*I'm so tired. Drained. Exhausted. Frazzled. I'm
running on empty with no end in sight.*

Help. I need help. Lots of help.

Parenting is a difficult, ongoing privilege and challenge. We want the best for our kids. We love them. We protect them.

Yet, there are some things that we can't protect them from. Loss is one of those things. The resulting heartache and grief are natural and real. They have to learn to navigate this.

Kids learn to handle the tough parts of life by watching their parents. How we respond to loss and difficulty profoundly influences them.

When we grieve in front of our kids – being honest and real – we send the message that loss is real, it hurts, and it's okay to show that. When we hide our grief in order to protect them, we send a message that this kind of pain should not be displayed or talked about.

Don't be afraid to show your emotions or to grieve in front of your kids. Being real with them (appropriate to their age, of course) is part of loving them. You're telling them that it's okay to grieve – and that's huge because they're grieving deeply and they don't know what to do with that.

Parenting requires tons of wisdom. Wisdom comes from God. He is the ultimate and perfect parent. Yield yourself to Him and ask Him to love and guide your kids. Seek His wisdom.

It's about getting this right. Who knows what that would be? It's not about getting it perfect. That's impossible. Parenting through grief is all about relying completely on God and loving our kids with the wisdom and strength He provides.

God is gracious to you. Be gracious to yourself. Parenting is always messy, especially while grieving.

Consider it pure joy, my brothers and sisters, whenever you face trials of many kinds, because you know that the testing of your faith produces perseverance. Let perseverance finish its work so that you may be mature and complete, not lacking anything. If any of you lacks wisdom, you should ask God, who gives generously to all without finding fault, and it will be given to you.
James 1:2-5

Lord, I give You myself again today. Give me Your wisdom. Love and parent my kids through me. They are Yours. Thank you for making me their parent.

100

As I read the Scriptures, I keep running across verses that say that Christ is in me and that I am in Him.

I've read these before, but they're hitting home with me now. He's not just with me, but in me. I'm not just with Him, but in Him.

I don't know what this means, but I want to accept it as true. It sounds safe and comforting. I want to experience this connection with God more.

At times, there seems to be a wide gap between what I feel and what Scripture says. I want to experience God Himself. I know I do, but I want more. I need more.

I want more of Him and His peace and joy amid all this trouble and grief. I desperately need His companionship to quell this terrible pain inside me.

All of us have a faith-experience gap. There are many things that we believe—or say we believe—that we don't experience much in daily life.

Simply put, we wonder if God is so good, why are things the way they are? Why do terrible things like the death of a child occur? If His love for us is perfect, why do we feel as we do?

We're restless. On some level we should be. There is a godly restlessness that occurs for many of us. We long to see our Creator face-to-face and be with Him completely. We hunger for heaven.

Our hopes and dreams usually reveal this longing. Our grief and pain express our thirst for eternity and for things to be as they should be. This world is not our home. We are citizens of heaven. God Himself is our home.

No wonder we yearn. It's a sort of holy discontent. As we walk with Him, we learn to experience more of Him here—His goodness, love, and comfort. We're content in Him, yet we long for more. We're longing for more of Him.

One day, we will be fully satisfied. For now, we yearn.

Dear friends, now we are children of God, and what we will be has not yet been made known. But we know that when Christ appears, we shall be like Him, for we shall see Him as He is.
1 John 3:2

When I see You, Lord, I will be whole and fully satisfied. Until then, I yearn. My heart looks for total and complete healing. I have that in You. One day I will experience it.

101

I still wonder why I'm here sometimes.

I know that's ridiculous, because I know why I'm here. God put me here.

I didn't decide to whom or when I would be born. I don't cause my own heart to beat or my brain to function. I don't control hardly anything.

The world feels so big, and I feel so small. Tiny. Powerful forces seem to be behind everything, driving events, situations, and people here and there.

When I realize this, I'm stunned. Most of the time I refuse to even go there. I keep my head down, focus on my own agenda, and don't concern myself with such things. All the big stuff seems instantly overwhelming.

Who am I in all this? How do I go on without my child? How do I make sense of this new life?

I wonder. A huge part of me is missing. I feel so lost sometimes.

The loss of a child causes us to think about a lot of things.

We see life and events differently. Our hearts have been tenderized. We're more sensitive to pain and suffering.

Even though we still find ourselves going through the motions, living on autopilot isn't good enough anymore. Deep down, we want to live. We want to matter. We want our lives to count. Part of our pain stems from a longing for heaven.

We're hungering for God. We're created by Him and for Him. He alone knows our true and complete purpose. He gives each of us a unique calling and mission.

Whatever the calling or mission, it comes down to loving Him and loving people. We're wired to love and be loved. You know this. Your love for your child is immense, deep, and strong.

God is love. He invites us to experience Him. He is at work in you. He will complete what He started. He is working in you today, even if you can't perceive it.

Being confident of this, that He who began a good work in you will carry it on to completion until the day of Christ Jesus.
Philippians 1:6

Lord, You are always at work in me. You will complete what You have started. I return to the basics today. I will focus on loving You by loving people. Work in and through me today.

102

I think I settle a lot.

I start out optimistic. I dream. I hope.

And then reality sets in and downgrades my expectations. I cease to hope for more and settle for what is.

I know accepting the current reality is important, but I miss my child desperately. I want them back. I still can't grasp a world without them.

But I don't want to grieve all the time. I want to live—and grieve well along the way.

I don't want to let this loss define me or determine my life.

I don't want to settle into some off-white, dull, small existence. I don't want to walk through life afraid of the next tragedy. I want to live and live well.

Those around me deserve this from me. How can I love others well if I'm stuck in grief?

We all seem to start as dreamers. Then we get disappointed, hurt, and wounded. Life begins to kick the optimism and imagination out of us. We become jaded. Careful. Cautious. Realistic.

In order to protect ourselves and those we love, we tighten our hearts. We try to control people and circumstances. We live our days guarded and hesitant. If we experience enough loss, we go internal. We hide.

We look at God differently too. Instead of a loving Father, He becomes a distant disciplinarian. Instead of intimate and deeply personal, we see Him as aloof and distracted—too busy with the grand affairs of the universe to pay too much attention to us.

After the death of a child, all of this gets kicked into high gear. Stress and grief squeeze our faith. We want to live and love others, but how do we do that when we can barely breathe?

Healing and growth begin with a sense of safety. When our personal worlds are upside down and our hearts are crushed, it's hard to feel safe and secure.

Faith and trust are inherently risky. Yet, if God is who He says He is, He is ultimate safety. Our challenge is to see Him for who He is, rather than letting our minds recreate Him in our image based on what's happened to us.

Only God Himself satisfies. Only He can give us true perspective. He is our strength, our healing, our hope, and our life.

Whom have I in heaven but you? And earth has nothing I desire besides you. My flesh and my heart may fail, but God is the strength of my heart and my portion forever.
Psalm 73:25-26

Lord, You are life. You are my home. All my longings are ultimately about You. Only you can meet my needs. Be my priority and my foremost desire.

103

I know God is good. That's what my mind tells me.

My heart is wounded. I can't feel His goodness sometimes, though I see it all around me.

The loss of my child has been heart-crushing. The emotional pain is deep and overwhelming.

I can see now why some consider self-medicating—or even suicide. Life can be heavy, and depressing.

I guess we all self-medicate, don't we? One way or another, we all do less-than-healthy things to help ourselves feel better—myself included.

I've wondered before if it's worth it. Yes, I've had suicidal thoughts in the past.

Hopelessness and despair can be powerful indeed.

Each of us carries personal pain. For some, the burden is heavy and crippling.

There are times when our losses pile up and threaten to crush us. When a child dies, parents experience multiple, heavy losses in rapid succession. Everything changes.

Our entire life web is affected and forever altered. Nothing will ever be the same.

Pain gets our attention. We're designed for relationship, not separation. We were created to connect and to love. Loss goes against the natural grain of our hearts.

Sadly, we live in a broken, loss-ridden, and pain-filled world. God wants to give us peace in Himself amid all the turmoil and upheaval.

Keep being real with Him. As much as possible, hide nothing. He knows anyway. Unburden your heart.

Breathe deeply and see yourself resting in God.

"Surely God is my salvation; I will trust and not be afraid. The Lord, the Lord Himself, is my strength and my defense; He has become my salvation."
Isaiah 12:2

I rest in You, Lord. Though I feel shaky and uncertain, You are my fortress and my strength. I release my fears and worries now, one by one.

104

I bounce around emotionally. I used to be stable. Now, I don't know.

One moment I can be okay and the next moment I'm a mess.

Sad. Relieved. Irritated. Delighted. Frustrated. Peaceful. Confused. Numb.

Since the loss of my child, I can be all of these, and much more, in the span of a couple of hours. I feel like I'm on a marathon roller coaster. Just hanging on is exhausting.

I feel settled about God and His love for me, and then my grief gets triggered and I'm suddenly wondering about everything again. Emotional upheaval has become my new normal.

I don't like all this unpredictability. I like stability, but the ground under me is constantly shifting. I have trouble keeping my footing.

I'm tired. Life and loss have worn me out.

The death of a child can shatter a parent's heart.

Our souls are shaken. The lid of our internal Pandora's box of feelings is blown off and out comes what appears to be a random, hodgepodge mixture of up-and-down and back-and-forth emotions.

We're more sensitive. We feel more vulnerable. Life as we knew it has tilted, cracked, or even disappeared. All this is confusing, disorienting, and frightening.

Nothing feels settled anymore, perhaps not even God and what we think or believe about Him. We're unsure of everything—of life, other people, ourselves, and even God.

Be real with Him. He knows every twitch of your heart, every thought that passes through your mind. He feels your loneliness and walks with you in it.

God loves you. Because of Jesus Christ and your trust in Him, God's acceptance of you is complete and total.

Breathe deeply. Though hard to imagine now, this emotional hijacking will diminish over time and eventually pass. Hang on. Trust.

God your Father is the ultimate parent. He feels your pain.

Your sun will never set again, and your moon will wane no more; the Lord will be your everlasting light, and your days of sorrow will end.
Isaiah 60:20

Help me remember, O Lord, that now is not forever. Things have changed and will continue to change, but You are always the same.

105

The loss of my child and my own issues are more than enough to deal with. I don't need everyone else's stuff on top of that.

The world is depressing. Trouble everywhere. People acting crazy.

I sense anger. I see anxiety in people's eyes. It's all too much. Too heavy for my small heart.

Maybe I'm thinking about things too much, but what's happening around me is hard to ignore. Can't we pause and let me catch my breath?

I can't handle my own life, much less any extras. My own obligations feel like Mount Everest. I'm learning to live in a constant state of fatigue, but I don't like it.

I miss my child. I feel like I need them here with me, now, more than ever.

We get bombarded with a stunning amount of information every day, and little of it is positive or uplifting. Problems abound. Life is tough. People are hurting.

We're hurting too – badly. When we're in pain, sometimes all we can see is pain. Our hearts have been broken open and every wind that blows through stirs our emotions.

Perhaps we feel the pain of others more acutely. We're learning empathy through suffering. This is a good thing but draining.

Feeling and sharing in the pain and suffering of others is part of love.

Your child is gone from your sight. The pain is deep. Your heart senses the pain of others around you. This can feel overwhelming.

You're designed to be a reflection of God and His love to those around you. He lives in you. He is up to the task. Even when fatigued and exhausted, God can work in and through you in wonderful ways.

Breathe deeply. Lean into Him. Pour out your heart to Him. Rest. Trust.

***Surely God is my help; the Lord is
the one who sustains me.
Psalm 54:4***

*No matter what happens to me or around me, Your love
for me is unchanged. You sustain me. You are my life.
I present myself to You. Use me today as You wish.*

106

I can't believe I'm about to say this. At times, I have trouble remembering what my child looked like. I'm also having trouble remembering what their voice sounded like.

This terrifies me.

When this happens, I rush to my phone and then to my computer. I look at old pictures. I watch a few videos.

How could I ever forget their face or their voice? What's happening? Am I that out-of-sight, out-of-mind?

I feel guilty all over again. I can't believe they're gone.

How can someone just disappear? Did all that really happen? Is this a dream?

If this is a dream, it's a nightmare. I'm ready to wake up.

Our child has a forever place in our hearts. When they depart, they leave a hole. That hole is reserved for them. We live on with a hole in our hearts.

We're designed by God for relationships. This is part of what it means to be human. What you're describing is common for grieving parents.

You're human. Like most of us, you tend to remember best what and who you're around the most. You're not forgetting your child. That's impossible. The loss is simply sinking into a deeper place in your heart.

You'll never forget them. Love endures.

On some level, you'll always grieve. You miss them, but the intensity of the missing will change over time. This is part of healing. You're not distancing yourself from your child. The Lord is healing your heart.

Breathe deeply. Your heart is still in pieces. Be patient with yourself. Lean into God. He carries you.

Love always protects, always trusts, always hopes, always perseveres. Love never fails.
1 Corinthians 13:7-8

Lord, no matter what I feel, Your love is perfect.
Thank you for loving me. Thank you giving me
the ability to love. I give this pain to You.

107

*I feel emotionally handicapped. My child is gone.
It feels like my heart left with them.*

I move in a fog. I'm tired and can't seem to get on top of life.

*My child is never far from my mind. I miss them
terribly. The hurt surfaces all over again.*

*Perhaps the pain is there all the time, just
waiting for an excuse to show itself.*

*I feel like a whiner. I despise it when others complain,
but here I am, spewing my stuff everywhere.*

*Is there a difference between whining and venting? Are
complaining and processing the same thing sometimes?*

*This is going to sound bizarre—I try to rest in God,
but I'm too tired. I have so much on my mind and
heart that I can't rest inside. My mind is spinning.
My heart is bouncing all over the place.*

Help.

Things have changed. Your world has been dramatically altered. Your heart is rattled and desperately trying to regain its balance. Your mind has been stunned and is frantically searching for resolution.

Your child is no longer physically with you. A huge, thick strand has been severed. Your life web is shaking.

Whether we call it whining, complaining, venting, or processing, it feels good and right to express our hearts—especially with those we feel safest with. Especially with God, the ultimate safe person.

God your Father welcomes you today. All of you. All of you with all the mess. He's in this with you—loving and guiding you in ways you are not aware of.

Yes, rest is hard when you're spinning in circles. Breathe deeply and know that God is with you, in you, even as you spin. This too will pass. Keep being real with Him.

For great is His love toward us, and the faithfulness of the Lord endures forever. Praise the Lord.
Psalm 117:2

No matter what my circumstances, Lord, You are with me. Even better, You are in me, and I am in You. I accept these truths today, even if I don't feel them much at present.

108

I want to experience God more. I want to be used by Him in the lives of others.

Honestly, however, what I want most right now is relief. I want peace. I want some answers. I want energy to do daily life. I want some space.

There is no space out there. My life doesn't allow it. Family, work, church, neighbors, finances—the list goes on and on.

All of me, all my time, all my energy accounted for and gobbled up before my feet hit the floor in the morning.

My child is gone. The heaviness of it all can be stifling.

I was busy before, but I didn't feel like this. I'm exhausted.

After the loss of a child, the resulting grief process is exhausting. Over time, fatigue skews our thinking. If sleep deprivation is the most basic form of torture, then long-term fatigue can have some debilitating results.

The answer is not to flee fatigue. We naturally feel what happens to us and around us. When a child dies, our hearts grieve deeply. That grief can take up huge amounts of space. Suddenly, life takes much more energy than before. Again, this is natural. Common. Normal.

Grief cannot be effectively avoided. It is meant to be felt and processed over time. Your heart is your most prized possession. It needs your patience and kindness right now.

Most of us have to do less when we're grieving. You're human and no exception to this. Your only task is to receive from God and walk with Him. He can handle your life. He can manage your responsibilities.

Breathe. Experience His presence and His love. He is your life, your soul's oxygen.

Truly my soul finds rest in God; my salvation comes from Him. Truly He is my rock and my salvation; He is my fortress, I will never be shaken.
Psalm 62:1-2

Lord, I seek You. Order my routine. Help me make decisions that build space into my life and heart. Refresh me, Lord.

109

I'm not at my best right now—far from it.

I believe in excellence. I'm used to giving it my all and doing things well.

I'm not sure I'm doing anything well right now.

My child is gone. I feel like a shadow of my former self.

I never knew loss could feel like this.

I guess I imagined grief would be more manageable, or perhaps more definable. I never expected this much upheaval and vulnerability.

I want to give God my best, but that's not much right now. I don't feel like I have anything to give.

You don't have to be at your best to experience God's love and goodness. You don't have to be on the top of your game for God to work through you and use you. You just need to be willing.

The truth is that God can work in and through us when we feel weak, powerless, and sad. He can use a broken and exhausted parent's heart to bring comfort and peace to others. He routinely shows Himself through our weaknesses and even what we think are failures.

He is teaching you. He is guiding you. He is expressing His

love for you, moment-by-moment. Yes, I know your feelings lag behind these realities. That's okay. Anchor yourself in God's facts, and your feelings will eventually catch up.

> *Therefore, since we have been justified through faith, we have peace with God through our Lord Jesus Christ.*
> ***Romans 5:1***

*On my worst day, Lord, You still love me completely.
I have peace with You, even when I do not feel it.
You live in me. Live through me, as You wish.*

110

Nothing feels right lately. I seem to be out of sync. Something's wrong.

Maybe it's all me. Perhaps I'm wrong.

The loss of my child has crushed me. I don't know which end is up.

And then perspective will come again. My heart will settle a little. I get some peace.

But then daily life chases it away. I'm glad to be busy, and yet I don't have time or energy to process much of anything.

The more fatigued I am, the more my mood rules me.

Feelings hijack me and begin to drive my life. My emotions can be so strong and powerful.

After the death of a child, our hearts are shattered. No wonder our emotions are spilling out everywhere and all over everything.

You're right. Emotions are powerful. In our world, we often get things backwards. Feelings rule. Mood is king. If it feels right, we think it's true. If it feels good, we believe it. Feelings can end up driving our faith.

God's growth process for us is the other way around. It begins with facts—things He has revealed about Himself, us, and life. We accept and believe these things, though at times our feelings might not totally line up with God's facts. As we let facts drive our faith, our feelings eventually begin to follow.

We are emotional beings. God created us this way. Our feelings are meant to be felt, but not necessarily bowed down to.

Be aware of your feelings. Acknowledge the emotions. Find ways to express what's happening inside you. Breathe deeply. Process what needs to be processed. As you do, the feelings will begin to take their proper place in the scheme of things.

I have been crucified with Christ and I no longer live, but Christ lives in me. The life I now live in the body, I live by faith in the Son of God, who loved me and gave Himself for me.
Galatians 2:20

My life is not about me. Lord, I give You my feelings. Focus me on You and Your truth. I want to live by faith. Immerse me in Your facts.

111

It's so strange.

Time marches on, but not for my child.
Time has stopped for them.

What I mean is that they will always be the same age they were when they died. At least, it will be so in my mind and heart.

It's as if part of the timeline of my life abruptly stopped when they took their final breath.

Now I know what other parents meant when they said, "They are forever 19, 47, 23, or 2."

I don't know how to think about this, and I sure don't know how to feel about it.

Maybe part of my heart is stuck back at the moment they died.

The rest of me is being forcefully sucked along by the world around me and its demands.

I live in two time zones.
I feel so torn and divided.

What you have just expressed is very common and natural for bereaved parents. When our child died, all of life changed in an instant. We now live in two worlds. This is confusing, frustrating, exhausting, and surreal.

That surreal feeling can last for a very long time. For most grieving parents, it comes and goes according to the day and what's happening in us and around us at any given moment.

The challenge is to somehow begin to accept this uncomfortable, living-in-two-time-zones reality for what it is. And this means accepting ourselves and whatever is happening inside us during this brutal roller-coaster-like grief marathon.

There are benefits to embracing the surreal. This loss can teach us what's really valuable in life. Our pain and grief can be used by God to empower us to live with more clarity, meaning, and purpose than ever before.

As followers of Jesus, we have always lived in two time zones: the temporal and the eternal. As human beings on this planet, we're typically far more attuned to the temporal here-and-now earthly reality immediate around us. The Bible tells us that there is another, deeper, and permanent reality all around us as well: the eternal. We live in both worlds at once.

God invites us to live fully here with our eyes fixed on Him and eternity. He calls us to embrace Him and eternity as our ultimate reality—our home. As we put on eternal glasses, we get a new perspective on life here.

We can't work our way into an eternal mindset. If we know Jesus, He lives in us. He already has a perfect, eternal perspective. As we walk with Him in His word, He teaches us. He transforms us. He renews our minds.

He knows your grief. He feels it with you. His arms are around you. Continue to release all to Him. He loves you.

Since, then, you have been raised with Christ, set your hearts on things above, where Christ is, seated at the right hand of God. Set your minds on things above, not on earthly things.
Colossians 3:1-2

*Lord, open the eyes of my heart to see more of the eternal.
Give me Your eyes. Teach me
in Your Word. Give me true perspective. You
are my comfort, my hope, my God.*

112

I've been thinking about the power of emotions. I do tend to give them too much credit and way too much influence in my life. They're important, but I don't want my feelings to be my guide and driving force in life.

Feelings can be beautiful. I have wonderful memories of my child. I smile at them.

Those same memories also bring tears. I'm deeply aware of what I've lost.

I'm thankful for all those memories, though right now they might bring pain. I think the pain is already inside me and the memories are gifts from God to help me release the pain and heal.

Why do life and loss have to be so emotional?

My feelings are such a jumble that sometimes I have difficulty knowing what I'm feeling at any given time.

This is all so confusing.

In grief and in life, we tend to let emotion drive our lives. We put feelings first and allow them to greatly influence or even determine what we do and what we believe.

Part of life's battle is to turn this around and let God's facts lead the way. As we know Him better, our faith forms and solidifies, and eventually our feelings follow.

Choosing to believe God and His facts, even when we're conflicted emotionally, grounds us—in a good way. He becomes our anchor. We're no longer tossed here and there by every wind of emotion that blows through. Gratitude surfaces. Memories become priceless treasures.

The loss of our child and the resulting pain can easily dominate our minds and hearts. As you feel the grief, keep expressing it to God and a few people you trust. Get the grief out.

As you grieve, begin to let your mind dwell on what is good. Embrace the memories. Feel the emotions. Process the thoughts. Feel your steady anchor. Jesus is right there with you, in you.

Breathe deeply and know you are safe.

Praise be to the God and Father of our Lord Jesus Christ, who has blessed us in the heavenly realms with every spiritual blessing in Christ.
Ephesians 1:3

No matter how I feel at any given moment, I have been blessed with every spiritual blessing in You, Lord. You are life. If I have You, I have everything.

113

I know I've said this before. One of the disconcerting results of losing my child is that it has introduced me to the stark reality that anything can happen to anyone at any time.

Even to me. Even to others I love and care about.

I don't feel as safe anymore. I stay busy and distracted, but in quieter moments the uncertainty of life descends on me like a load of bricks.

I figure it's better to admit these thoughts and get them out there. The alternative is to ignore and bury them. I choose to expose them in the hopes that they won't take root and produce fruit that doesn't help me or those around me.

Are my loved ones safe? Am I safe? How safe?

What is safety, anyway?

To heal and grow, we need a sense of safety. When a child dies, our sense of security can be deeply shaken. We can begin living in fight-or-flight mode. Fear, rather than faith, can become the fuel that propels us.

I think again of Psalm 23. Even though we walk through the dark, unfamiliar, and frightening territory of child loss, we need not fear. Our Shepherd is with us. He guides and protects. He heals and leads. He carries us. He surrounds us.

We live in an imperfect and broken world where pain and loss appear to rule at times. Death can give us perspective. This life is not all there is. God uses this life to introduce us to eternity and train us for heaven.

We are forever beings, created by God for God. He feels our pain. He comforts us.

Jesus knows all about pain, grief, sorrow, and suffering. He has experienced death. He died for us, in our place. He gave His life for us so that He might live His life in us and through us.

Life is about Him. He is life. He is ultimate safety. When our eternal, spiritual safety begins to be more important than earthly, physical safety, we begin to experience some of the freedom that He promises us.

See yourself leaning into Him today. Because of Jesus and your trust in Him, know that you are forever spiritually safe.

You are my strength, I watch for You; You, God, are my fortress, my God on whom I can rely.
Psalm 63:6-8

Lord, when I don't feel safe, move my heart to seek You. Let me know You are with me. Let me experience Your love and safety.

114

If God is ultimate safety, and I know Him, how come I don't feel safe? Why do I worry about my loved ones? Is it because I'm missing my child so desperately?

Wait. I'm back to feelings again, aren't I? If God tells me I'm safe, then I'm safe, no matter what I might feel.

Perhaps I'm confusing physical safety with ultimate, spiritual safety. It's hard for me to separate the two.

My feelings are valid, but they aren't always reality. I trust that God is true and right. He has me. I am safe—eternally safe.

The more I believe I'm eternally safe and trust what God has said, the more I will begin to feel it.

Facts, faith, and then feelings.

I think I'm getting it.

In the heat of the battle, all this flies out the window. I'll let that be okay and trust that God is training me over time. Growth and healing take time, don't they?

I'm so impatient sometimes.

Living life well begins with knowing the truth. God Himself is ultimate truth. All truth flows from Him. He is life. When we embrace Him as our life, things begin to make more sense.

The Bible is full of verses about our safety. God is faithful.

He is committed. He is love. He doesn't forsake or abandon. Unthinkable tragedies may happen, but we are eternally and spiritually safe in Him.

Picture yourself in Him. Scripture says if you've trusted in Christ, He lives in you and you in Him. All things have been created by Him and for Him and through Him and in Him all things hold together. He is perfect. His safety is perfect.

In this world, we will have trouble—lots of it. He has overcome the world.

You live in Him. He lives in you. You are loved. You are safe.

The Lord will guide you always; He will satisfy your needs in a sun-scorched land and will strengthen your frame. You will be like a well-watered garden, like a spring whose waters never fail.
Isaiah 58:11

No matter how things might seem, You love me perfectly. I am safe and secure in You. You are safety and security. Help me to trust You.

115

Life is a struggle. The routine is merciless and demanding. Nothing slows down to allow for pain and loss – not even for a child's death.

Everyone is busy about their business, unaware of the grief around them. Perhaps most people are unaware of their own grief. Maybe they don't want to face it.

I can understand that. Ignoring it sounds good, but that is not the path of healing. I would be hiding from myself and God.

I see sadness in the eyes of others now. I believe my support group has a lot to do with this.

Being with others who are openly grieving gives my heart room to feel, emote, and vent. The release is good, and probably more important than I realize.

As I verbalize and process my own loss and grief, there seems to be more space in my heart to see others.

I miss my child desperately. I always will. But the pain is different. It's a shared pain somehow.

*I've let others in.
And I'm willing for others to let me in.*

We're designed by God for relationship. We're wired for connection with Him and with other people.

Loss and separation are hard and painful – especially the death of a child. When we're able to authentically share our pain and be heard, we feel loved. When we experience love, we heal a little bit.

God is love. Even if all others avert their faces and avoid us, we're still the ongoing recipients of perfect, limitless love. We can't feel the full delight of this, but we can taste minuscule bits of it, and those little bits of perfect love add up over time.

Some of us are more isolated than others. I believe, however, that God places safe, loving people around us. We just need eyes to see them and hearts receptive enough to engage.

Many bereaved parents attempt to ignore and stuff their grief, but it will always be expressed, one way or another. It doesn't go away. Grief is meant to be felt.

You've said it well. Our pain is a shared pain.

There is One who feels what we feel. He knows. He understands. Even if there are times we can't feel it, He is still the Father of compassion and the God of all comfort.

---

*You are my refuge and my shield; I
have put my hope in your word.
Psalm 119:114*

Many are hurting, Lord. You are hope and healing. Move hearts to seek You. Make me more aware of You. Let me see You everywhere.

116

When I talk to other grieving parents, we all seem to be experiencing frustration in our relationships. I know I've talked about this before, but I need to vent a little.

People we counted on disappeared. People avoid us. People act like we've got some infectious disease. People don't seem to know what to do with us, even though they too have experienced loss in life of some kind.

I don't get it. Can't people just be kind and compassionate? What's so hard about that?

I now know quite a few people who feel rejected and abandoned by friends, co-workers, and even family. People they thought cared about them and who promised support.

Frustrating.

This adds insult to injury. The death of our children was more than enough. None of us needed more loss on top of that.

People react to deep loss and intense grief in strange ways.

You're right. Every person has experienced loss and pain. And yet our willingness and ability to connect with and love others when they're hurting seems severely limited.

Perhaps there's a basic human principle operating here. We avoid pain. Our own pain. Others' pain. The world's pain.

We've had enough and seen enough. We don't want any more, so we pretend it's not there.

We're all imperfect and fallible. We're prone to fear, selfishness, and self-protection. Our heart space is limited, and if we haven't grieved prior losses in healthy ways, we will not respond well to loss in the lives of those around us—especially the terrible loss of a child. We'll make light of it, try to fix it, or run.

Developing the skill of forgiveness is more important than any of us can truly appreciate. God knows all about being ignored, rejected, and betrayed. He experiences these things continually. We're in good company.

Christ is with you. He lives in you. He is an expert at forgiveness. Lean into Him. Trust. Release offenses and burdens to Him.

Finally, brothers and sisters, rejoice! Strive for full restoration, encourage one another, be of one mind, live in peace. And the God of love and peace will be with you.
2 Corinthians 13:11

You, Lord, are the forgiveness expert. You live in me. Enable me to forgive quickly. Love those around me through me, even while my heart is shaking.

117

I want to talk more about people and relationships.

I find myself getting angry, not just for myself, but for other bereaved parents and how they're being treated by the world and those immediately around them. People can be cold. Mean. Even unfeeling.

I don't understand. How can they be like that? And many of them call themselves Christians. How can this be?

Going to church has been hard at times. It stirs my heart to the depths, and I'm very aware of who's missing.

The empty space in my heart is a constant reminder of my child. Some people are supportive, but some aren't. Most don't seem to know what to do with me.

Other grieving parents I talk to express the same things. People just stare. They blabber something belittling and then walk away. Or they avoid us altogether.

No wonder I feel so alone.

One of our general expectations in life is that we should be treated with kindness and respect. If not this, at least some common human decency would be appreciated.

Someone has said that an expectation is a disappointment waiting to happen. After the death of a child, we're more vulnerable and certainly expect the usual engagement and kindness. When that doesn't happen, we feel robbed, cheated, and even abused.

At some point, we come to the place where we decide whether our expectations of others are realistic. And even if they are realistic, are we setting ourselves up for disappointment by having these expectations in the first place?

Releasing those around us from our usual expectations helps guard our hearts at this tender time. This can also turn our attention away from people's reactions and toward God's love and understanding. Releasing our expectations of those around us can also motivate us to pursue safe people who know grief well.

Look to the Lord. He understands rejection. He experiences it all the time.

God is your life, your hope, and your safety. He will never leave you or forsake you. He is your constant companion.

But we have this treasure in jars of clay to show that this all-surpassing power is from God and not from us. We are hard pressed on every side, but not crushed; perplexed, but not in despair...
2 Corinthians 4:7-8

There are times, Lord, when some relationships seem impossible. I will guard my heart and trust You. Help me to release those around me of any unrealistic expectations I might have.

118

I've been moaning about the lack of compassion in the world. I've judged those around me for their lack of understanding. And then a friend reminded me that I wasn't the most compassionate soul on the planet when they lost their child.

I was stunned. I thought I was being supportive. I didn't realize how I was coming across.

Turns out that I was guilty of most of what I've been judging others for. This was humbling, but good.

At first, I was mad. Then I accepted the truth.

I'm far from perfect. I have been guilty at some time or other of most of what I complain about in others.

I'm sorry, Lord. I confess this to you. I feel guilty.

What you've said is true for most of us. We're guilty—either now or in the past—of most of what irritates us in others.

Ever since the Garden of Eden, we've been complaining about the behavior of others and trying to fix their issues rather than looking at our own hearts and dealing with ours. We have no right or place to judge, and yet we do.

When confronted with our lack of love and compassion, we typically either laugh it off and keep judging others, or we allow the truth to humble us. God's goal is not to mire us in guilt, but rather free us of unhealthy thoughts and actions.

God is love. He is eager to love us by loving others through us. When we judge, we block this process.

God's forgiveness is complete. Jesus' sacrifice for us is perfect. Instead of wallowing in guilt, we confess. We receive God's forgiveness. We get up and allow Him to love through us. This brings healing, both to others and our own hearts.

Blessed are the merciful, for they will be shown mercy. Blessed are the pure in heart, for they will see God. Blessed are the peacemakers, for they will be called children of God.
Matthew 5:7-9

Lord, you are merciful. You live in me. Extend Your love and mercy through me to all around me. I want to be pure in heart – a peacemaker.

119

After yesterday's gentle confrontation, I remembered more about how I responded to people in the past in times of loss.

I've complained about the unhelpful things that others have said to me. I've probably said the same things myself. I didn't understand, and I was running from their pain rather than meeting them in it.

I'm trying to release the guilt when it comes, focus on God's forgiveness, and learn from this.

I'm determined now to be different. I'll be compassionate.

I'll be part of God's comfort for hurting people.

I'll try to be more merciful toward those who disappear, critique, judge, and say unhelpful things. I'll pray for them. They have pain too.

The death of my child is teaching me many things. Lord, use all this for good—somehow, someway.

We're all guilty of most of what we dislike in others. Perhaps we see ourselves and are expressing our frustration that we are the way we are.

We all run from pain. After all, who would run toward it?

And yet, Jesus, knowing what was ahead of Him, resolutely fulfilled His mission and laid down His life for us.

Jesus lives in us. He wants to live through us and express His sacrificial love.

We are His ambassadors and emissaries of His comfort and healing. We can enter others' lives and meet them where they are— in all the mess. This is an honor and a privilege.

We can give away what we have received—love, forgiveness, patience, kindness, comfort. Such compassion comes from the Lord Himself. Walk with Him in the present moment. He is your help and healing.

We are therefore Christ's ambassadors, as though
God were making His appeal through us.
2 Corinthians 5:20

Lord, I receive Your forgiveness for the unkind things
I have thought and said when others were in pain.
I am Your ambassador.
Live through me in compassion to others.

120

I want to make a difference. I want to use all this pain and grief for good.

I keep thinking I need to be doing better to be of any help to others. Have I healed enough to be of any benefit?

I don't know.

When is enough healing enough? What does "doing better" look like now?

When have I progressed enough that I can be used by God to bring solace and comfort to others?

I try, but sometimes my own grief gets in the way. Their pain triggers mine. I can make things about myself again in a heartbeat.

I miss my child desperately. I want this grief and loneliness to count somehow.

Thankfully, we don't have to be doing well for God to use us. He delights in expressing His love to and through us when we're at our worst and weakest.

Life is not something we can plan and expect to work out as we have envisioned. After losing your child, you know this all too well. We don't know what's going to happen or when.

Loving God, ourselves, and others is a dynamic, moment by

moment, ever-changing process. Our best bet is to simply stay focused on God as much as possible.

We're constantly receiving all good things from Him. As we walk with Him, we naturally give away what we have received—love, goodness, comfort, compassion, etc.

As our grief gets triggered, we grieve together with those we're serving. It's not about getting it right. It's about giving and receiving love. It's about receiving what God has for us and letting Him live through us to those around us.

God is always at work. He is the Comforter. He lives in you. He will live through you today.

For we are God's handiwork, created in
Christ Jesus to do good works, which God
prepared in advance for us to do.
Ephesians 2:10

You thought of me, wanted me, and created me. I am Your handiwork. I will rest in You and trust that You work in and through me for Your good pleasure.

121

This grief journey seems so long and challenging. Every day brings reminders. I miss my child terribly.

I'm thankful for my support group. I'm grateful for the people who love me amid all my personal chaos. They're not perfect. They mess up from time to time. I do too. We're in it together.

A safe person's presence is powerful. It's easier to believe God loves me when people do.

I'm finding ways to get around helpful people more and limit my exposure to unhelpful or toxic influences. I'm learning to guard my heart. That feels good.

I need inspiring, encouraging, and compassionate souls in my life. I'm healing, but I still need lots of understanding and acceptance.

I guess I need that all the time, don't I?

Love and acceptance are like oxygen to our souls, especially after the death of a child. We need a sense of safety to heal and grow. People who give us this gift are treasures indeed.

It's good to be aware of where we are. We're on the grief path. As we process our pain, we begin to heal. Healing takes time.

Our wounds can be deep. There are plenty of ups and downs and unforeseen obstacles on this path. We get surprised from time to time. We need patience from ourselves and from others.

God often reveals Himself through the presence and actions of safe, loving people. He teaches us to guard our hearts. He heals us, though we are never the same. We grow.

Along the way, if we're willing, God teaches us to be safe people—people who listen and act with compassion and empathy. We become people who can walk with others in their pain without making it about ourselves.

Keep letting God bring healing to your heart and mind. He is good. He loves you.

Be devoted to one another in love. Honor one another above yourselves.
Romans 12:10

Lord, help me to be real with You, myself, and other people. Give me the reassurance I need. Plant Your patience in me and cause it to grow.

122

I've mentioned before how hard it is to go to church now.

Don't get me wrong. I enjoy it. Well, parts of it. I want to be there. But it's not like it was.

My child is no longer here, and everything seems to remind me of them—including church.

My heart is different now. I'm different. Grief seems to hit me at church more than any other singular place.

Some ask me how I'm doing. Others avoid me. I feel like I'm wearing a sign, "Grieving parent. Approach at your own risk."

I need the connection, but I find myself wanting to get in and get out as quickly as possible. I want to be there, but I don't want to have to manage all these nutty emotions the entire time.

What do I do with all this?

When we go to worship with others, we naturally go to open our hearts and connect with God and others. The music, prayers, and message are designed to speak to our hearts and souls.

Your heart has been deeply wounded. Your soul may feel a bit battered, even shaky. You've been hit hard by the loss of your child. Your heart is cracked, and emotion naturally spills out everywhere.

Ideally, a gathering of other believers is a safe place. However, certain cultural expectations of what's appropriate and what's not come into play when we walk through the door. No matter what's happening inside, happy smiles proclaiming the message "I'm great!" are the usual fare.

Because you're hurting, you might feel out of sync. This is natural and common. Let it be what it is.

Take care of your own heart as best you can. Let church be, as much as possible, about the Lord. Breathe deeply and listen for His voice. He is with you, next to you, in you.

Because your love is better than life, my lips will glorify you. I will praise you as long as I live, and in your name I will lift up my hands.
Psalm 63:3-4

Set my heart on You, Lord. I am far too distracted by how I feel about what's happening around me. Set my mind on heavenly things.

123

I've concluded that it's okay if I'm uncomfortable in church. After all, how could I not be uncomfortable?

My child is gone. My heart is broken. My life is completely different. I feel lonely and out of sync with everyone else.

Uncomfortable doesn't mean bad. It just means uncomfortable.

Honestly, I'm uncomfortable almost anywhere and everywhere right now.

Looking back, it was in the uncomfortable times that I matured and grew spiritually. That doesn't mean I like it, but it certainly seems to be the truth.

I know there may be times at church that are particularly difficult. I'll be patient with myself and loving toward myself during those moments. If I need to step out or leave, so be it. That's okay.

The Lord knows my heart. He knows I love Him. He knows I want to be with Him.

He knows I need His Word, His comfort, and the fellowship with others. He knows.

I want to trust Him.

Yes, He knows.

And you're right: we rarely grow when we're comfortable. Comfort zones feel good, but they don't bring comfort.

Instead, they anesthetize our hearts. When all is well and no trouble is visible on the horizon, we tend to settle into mediocrity and small living.

God calls us to something greater: Faith.

You're trusting God as you walk in this deep valley of child loss. He honors this. He delights in your worship, adoration, and trust.

He is with you, in you, as you face feeling isolated and less than happy amid all the smiling Sunday faces. He walks the halls with you. He occupies your seat with you. He loves and accepts you as you are.

Yes, uncomfortable is okay. Focus on abiding in Him. Make Him your home no matter where you are or what you're doing. He is your life. He is your Shepherd.

The Sovereign Lord is my strength; He makes my feet like the feet of a deer; He enables me to tread on the heights.
Habakkuk 3:19

Though life might be uncomfortable, I will trust that You are guiding and leading. You love me. I will rest in Your love and receive from You.

124

If I can stop making things about me, I do so much better.

For example, when I go out in public, instead of concerning myself with how things are going to go and how others will respond to me, I try to focus on seeing others. I want to intentionally take an interest in each person that engages with me.

I want to take the spotlight off myself and place it where it should be—on those around me.

My child is gone, but I'm still here. I'm here to love. I'm here to do good. I'm here to be a reflection of my Father in heaven.

I wish I could do this consistently. I feel like an infant learning to move or stand up. I totter and fall a lot. I go back to crawling because it's what I know.

Making everything about me is as natural as breathing. It feels good when I get out of my own head and notice what and who's around me.

I feel like I'm living again, at least a little.

We live in a selfie world where we're encouraged to make everything about us.

Imagine a city street full of people all taking selfies. They smile, laugh, and pose, but no one is aware of what's happening around them. No one is connecting. Everyone is self-focused, living in their own head.

Sadly, that's close to reality.

As humans, we come out of the womb self-focused and then develop self-centeredness into our own personal art form. We make life all about us. God meant for life to be so much more.

I'm proud of you. Love begins with turning our hearts outward. It starts with setting our minds on the Lord and on engaging authentically with the world around us.

You are indeed a reflection of your Father. You were created in His image, and then recreated in Christ. You are a new creation now. Jesus lives in you, and He is love.

The more you accept what He has said about you, the more you will experience His love for you. As you trust Him, He lives and loves through you.

Do nothing out of selfish ambition or vain conceit. Rather, in humility value others above yourselves, not looking to your own interests but each of you to the interests of the others.
Philippians 2:3-4

Live through me, Lord.
Love those around me through me. Make each
day count. Let my life be about You.

125

This morning, I found myself reading in 1 Corinthians 13 – a passage about love. I smiled and thought of my child. As I read, the tears began to flow.

Love is patient and kind. It doesn't envy or boast. It's not proud or self-centered. It doesn't run others down or hold grudges.

It sees evil for what it is. It rejoices in the truth.

Love protects, trusts, hopes, perseveres, and never fails.

I always thought this is how I should be. And it is. But today I realized that these verses describe God's love. This is how He loves me. He is for me, always seeking my good.

I've been bogged down by grief and circumstances. Life without my child has been painful and heavy. Grief has worn me out.

And yet, I'm loved. I'm loved with a perfect love by a perfect Father.

I miss my child terribly, but I can rest in my Father's love.

The death of a child can lead us to appreciate love even more. Our pain can remind us to look to Him who is love – God Himself. We were created to experience God and His perfect love and then reflect Him and His love to others.

When we know and begin to believe that we are loved by Him (and begin to live like we're perfectly loved by a perfect Father), our lives make some dramatic shifts. We begin living outside ourselves and our own heads. We begin to flee from comparison and other dangers to our hearts. We immerse ourselves in what God has said about Himself, us, others, and life.

The better we know Him, the more we naturally reflect Him. The more we know and trust Him, the more He expresses Himself in and through us.

Over time, we become more of who we were meant to be—who we really are. New creations. Children of the King. Heirs of an Eternal Father.

Receive His love. Bask in it. Release all worries and fears into His capable hands. Immerse yourself in Him.

This is love: not that we loved God, but that he loved us and sent His Son as an atoning sacrifice for our sins.
1 John 4:10

I receive Your love today. Fill me. Let your love build in me and then flow out of me onto all those around me. Love through me, Lord.

126

I woke up this morning thinking about God's love. I realized that I haven't felt it as much as I would like to.

When my child died, I think I somehow distanced myself from God. Apparently, I tie His love to my circumstances. If things are going well, it's easier for me to say that He loves me. If things are hard or painful, I wonder what's wrong and where He is in all this.

My circumstances change, but He does not.

Do I see Him as responsible for all the painful stuff? I don't think so, but then I act like He's stopped blessing me and has turned His back on me somehow.

I'm sorry, Lord.

I miss my child. Life seems completely different now, and I don't like it. My feelings about You seem to vary with each passing breeze.

We tend to be emotion-driven creatures. If we like what's happening, we talk about God's love and goodness. In times of loss and confusion, we wonder where He went and why He allowed this to happen.

Breathe deeply. You're human. You're imperfect, fallible, and limited. You're enduring a massive loss – the death of your beloved child.

God has you. The fact that you are thinking about these things is proof that He is working in your mind and heart.

The road of life is full of unpleasant, unexpected events and situations. God is still your shepherd. His love for you is unwavering. He is leading, protecting, and blessing you, moment by moment.

There will be difficult places we must pass through, but there will be more green pastures ahead. It's about trust. As we learn to trust Him in times of uncertainty, our hearts open up to experience His love in those times.

You're learning. He's training you in faith and trust. You're growing. He knows your heart. His love for you is perfect and unchanging. And there's nothing you can ever do to cause Him to love you any more or any less.

For you created my inmost being; you knit me together in my mother's womb. I praise you because I am fearfully and wonderfully made; your works are wonderful, I know that full well.
Psalm 139:13-14

You thought of me and wanted me.
You created me in my mother's womb. I belong to You.
Your love for me is perfect.
Reassure me of Your love, Lord.

127

I'm still thinking about how closely I tie how I feel about what's happening to me and around me to God's love for me.

I guess I see God's love as either fickle or conditional.

It's frustrating. I know the issue is with me.

I can either believe and trust that God's love for me is perfect, or I can focus on my circumstances and emotions. I can let His truth rule my heart or allow myself to be blown about by every new wind of mood and emotion.

I'm frustrated with myself. Am I that addicted to feeling good? Is my hunger for comfort and pleasant circumstances that strong?

At the same time, I do want to feel better. I feel lonely and sad. I miss my child, but I'm tired of grief.

Then again, I feel guilty if I'm joyful about anything right now. Joy feels good, but wrong. How can anything be right when my child is not here?

Frustrating. Confusing. Weird.

If we're honest, most of us see ourselves as the center of the universe. We don't say that, but we think and act that way. We view life through the lens of self.

This greatly colors and perhaps even determines how we see hardship, loss, and emotional pain. We don't like it, therefore it's bad and to be avoided. If we're uncomfortable, we think something is wrong.

We tend to see God and His love through the lens of self too. No wonder we're confused, frustrated, and even angry.

God encourages us to change our lenses. He longs for us to see things as they are.

As we make Him, His love, and His Word our lens, our perspective begins to change. We begin to get the message that life involves us, but it's not about us.

The universe is designed to reveal Jesus Christ. He lives in you. He wants to be your lens, your life.

You're enduring the loss of your child. What could be more confusing and painful than this?

Continue to be real with your Lord about what's happening in your heart. He loves you. He is in you. You are in Him. He is closer than you know.

For in Him all things were created: things in heaven and on earth, visible and invisible, whether thrones or powers or rulers or authorities; all things have been created through Him and for Him. He is before all things, and in Him all things hold together.
Colossians 1:16-17

I embrace the truth that life is about You.
Everything owes its existence to You.
You are the center and focus. Lord, You are
my life. Be my center and my focus.

128

My child's birthday is coming up. What am I going to do?

I can't celebrate, can I? Wouldn't that be wrong, irreverent, disrespectful or something?

It hurts to even think about this. I would rather the day just disappear from the calendar.

I'm smart enough to know that sitting around and dreading the day's relentless approach isn't going to do me or anyone else any good. Yet, I'm clueless.

I feel a little paralyzed. I can feel the grief welling up inside me.

How do I celebrate the day they were born when they're dead?

Just thinking about this is excruciating. It brings everything back again.

Birthdays are special indeed. Your child's birthday is forever enshrined in your heart. It should be.

God thought about your child before He created the earth and the world. He determined the time and place where they would be born and live. He personally knit them together in the womb.

The day of your child's birth was clearly written on His divine calendar. It was a special day indeed when your precious child—a unique, created-in-God's-image, one-of-a-kind individual of priceless, eternal value—took their first breath.

Use the day to honor them. Make a simple plan that involves remembering them. Light a candle in their honor. Give a donation in their name. Buy a card and write to them. Find ways to express your love and what you miss.

Write to God, telling Him what you miss and how you feel. Speak your child's name out loud and talk about them to someone. Go through a photo album, thanking God for your child and all they were and are to you. Have a simple gathering and invite others to share and tell stories.

I know all this might sound emotional and scary. Remembering our children and celebrating their lives brings healing to our hearts.

Let God be the focus of your remembering. This helps put loss, death, grief, and life in perspective.

You discern my going out and my lying down; you are familiar with all my ways. Before a word is on my tongue you, Lord, know it completely.
Psalm 139:3-4

Lord, You know me. You know my heart and my grief. Be my comfort. Make this birthday count. Use it to bring healing and hope to my shaky soul.

129

*Thinking about my child's birthday triggered more fears
about other days lurking ahead on the calendar.*

*Thanksgiving. Christmas. Valentine's Day.
The anniversary of their death.*

I feel like the Grinch. I want to stop these days from coming.

*I need to change my attitude somehow. It does no good
to hunker down in dread. I want to turn this around
and use these days to help me grieve and heal.*

*Surely, these times can be part of God's plan
for me and those around me.*

*I can't yet imagine it, but I'm sure He can use
these days for good—for me and for everyone
who knew and cared about my child.*

Yes, He can. He will. These days are special to Him too. He knows them well.

He knows your heart and mind and all you're grappling with as time moves on. He feels your grief and pain. He wants to use these special times to express His love for you.

Birthdays, holidays, and anniversaries can be hard. We love. We experience heavy loss. We grieve. We heal as we remember and continue to express our love, trusting God as we travel this path of grief.

As special days approach, deal with the dread and anxiety by taking action. Make a simple plan. Intentionally honor your child and express your love for them. Involve others if possible. Talk about your child, share, and celebrate their life.

These holidays and special seasons will be forever different now, but they can still be good. Keep sharing with God what's happening inside you. He loves you. He is with you and is guiding you through this.

Love always protects, always trusts, always hopes, always perseveres. Love never fails.
1 Corinthians 13:7-8

Love endures. Lord, express Your love through me on these special days. Reassure me and heal me. I will trust You by making simple plans to love and honor my child.

130

My child's birthday was better than I expected.

I woke up nervous. I was anxious all morning. I set up a picture and then placed the card I bought in front of it.

In the card, I placed a letter I wrote. In the letter I talked about what I miss. I didn't edit. I simply wrote what I was thinking and feeling.

I read the letter out loud. It was hard. It was emotional. But it was good. I felt relieved afterward.

Later we gathered as a family and some others came over too. I asked everyone to get a birthday card and write in it whatever they wanted. We opened cards one by one, and people read what they wrote.

It was hard, but delightful. We got to grieve together. And I was able to grieve on my own too.

It turned out to be a good day.

I'm proud of you. You were intentional. You made a plan. You expressed your grief and what was happening inside you. You involved others. You gave them a tremendous gift by inviting them to grieve with you.

You remembered your child. You celebrated their life. You spoke their name and shared their story. You honored them on their birthday. That took courage and faith. Well done.

As we honor those the Lord has placed in our lives, we honor Him. We acknowledge Him as the planner and creator of the universe, ourselves, and all those we care about and love. We acknowledge that He created our children. He placed them in our lives and us in theirs.

When we remember our children, we also look ahead to the great reunion that is still in front of us. It will be a wonderful day indeed. We lean forward into eternity a little more. Our hearts remind us that this world is not our ultimate home.

Since you call on a Father who judges each person's work impartially, live out your time as foreigners here in reverent fear.
1 Peter 1:17

You thought of me and planned me long before I was born. I am not from here.
I am from You. This world is not my home. You are my home. Give me eternal perspective, Lord.

131

*I'm thankful my child's birthday went well.
It was emotional and draining.*

I'm exhausted, but it's a good kind of exhaustion. I honored them and expressed my love. That felt good.

I'm more hopeful now about the other special days ahead—Thanksgiving, Christmas, and my child's death anniversary. I'm going to make a plan, involve other people, and honor them as much as possible.

Love doesn't die. I knew that intellectually, but now I know it in my heart.

I still love my child. I always will. I can express that, even though they're not here with me.

I want to give God His place in all this. Without Him, my child would never have been here, and neither would I.

He is good. Life and love are gifts from Him.

Much of our angst about grief has to do with the unknown. We don't know what's coming next, how things will work out, or who we will be on the other side of this pain and loss. Being able to be proactive and plan for holidays and special times feels good. We're taking steps and making decisions to grieve well.

You're right. Love doesn't die. We're created in God's image.

We are eternal people. In our basic identity, we are spirits who have souls housed in bodies. This life is just the beginning, the preface, the introduction.

When we love, we honor Him who is love. When we honor our children, we honor the One who thought of them, planned them, created them and placed them in our lives.

Fundamentally, our lives are about Him. His plan involves us, but it's not about us. When we choose to place Him first, life begins to make more sense. We don't understand everything, of course, but we learn to trust more and more with each passing day.

***Many are the plans in a person's heart, but
it is the Lord's purpose that prevails.
Proverbs 19:21***

*Lord, You are life. You are my life. Your will be done in my
life as it is in heaven. My life is ultimately about You.*

132

This morning I realized that I've been thinking and acting like a victim. I saw all this as something that happened to me. I think somewhere deep inside, I blamed God.

I reasoned, "He could have stopped it. This didn't have to happen. Why did He take my child?"

Rationally, I know that God doesn't cause all things. That would make Him the author of evil and suffering. We live in a broken world where unspeakable and painful things happen.

Why us? Why them? Why me? Why then? These questions are too big for me, but my heart churns on them incessantly.

I must come to the point of accepting what I can't understand. Otherwise I'm choosing a life of anger, frustration, guilt, and more pain.

It's not so much what happened, but how I see it and what I do with it that seems to matter most now.

Lord, empower me. Renew my mind.

The lenses we look through make all the difference. We see tragedy. We experience pain, suffering, and deep loss. We can lose ourselves in asking, "Where is God in all this?"

With the lens of faith, we don't ignore this question, but we can choose to see the world more as God does. We live in a broken place full of challenges, loss, anxiety, and fear. Amid this bleak environment, God is at work expressing His love and care. He is busy bringing hope, healing, and triumphant good out of disaster.

Part of the Serenity Prayer expresses this well: "Living one day at a time, enjoying one moment at a time; accepting hardship as a pathway to peace; taking, as Jesus did, this sinful world as it is, not as I would have it; trusting that You will make all things right..."

We are heading to a place where everything is as it should be. This world, however, is not that place. God offers us His companionship and peace amid the present turmoil. He walks with you in this terrible valley of child loss. He makes all the difference.

Cast all your cares on Him. Release all things to Him. Rest in Him. See yourself in Him. He has you. His love for you is perfect.

My heart is not proud, Lord, my eyes are not haughty; I do not concern myself with great matters or things too wonderful for me. But I have calmed and quieted myself, I am like a weaned child with its mother; like a weaned child I am content.
Psalm 131:1-3

Lord, renew me and transform my thinking. Give me more of an eternal perspective. Speak to me. I rest in You. You are my life.

133

Well, I got the "aren't-you-over-this-yet?" eye roll again yesterday.

I've gotten that a lot. I decided to talk about my child, even if others were reluctant to bring them up. Hardly anyone mentions them. Instead of waiting to hear their name from others' lips, I decided to start speaking it myself.

Thankfully, some people have responded well. I find that if I share positively, rather than simply emoting, people are more able to listen and take it in. A few of them have joined in and shared of their loss and pain.

But I still get those eye rolls sometimes. I guess that's inevitable. I'm trying not to take it personally. I need to remember that their reaction is about them and not about me or my child.

Perhaps I scare them. I can imagine the thought of losing a child is as terrifying to them as it was to me.

Most people are compassionate and will give us a chance to grieve—for a while. Then, they expect us to be back to normal. By normal, I mean back to the way we were before. Of course, that's impossible. We're not the same people anymore.

What parent could be the same after the death of their child?

No, this loss changes everything about our lives. It changes us forever.

We struggle. We grieve. There are times when we wonder whether we can survive this.

Then our love for our child begins to express itself not only in pain, but in sharing, remembering, and memorializing. We become committed to honoring them through compassionate service.

Over time, we adjust, heal, and grow. We're not the same as before, and we shouldn't be.

I'm glad you've decided to grieve well, speak your child's name, talk about them, and let the world respond however it wants to. You've discovered a key truth. When we share positively—things like good memories and pleasant stories—people tend to respond better. Many times, your sharing will encourage others to share about their losses. This is healing for everyone.

As you honor God with your grief and sharing, you'll sense His companionship and blessing. He is empowering you to grieve well and live well. This honors your child—and the Lord who created them.

Shout for joy, you heavens; rejoice, you earth; burst into song, you mountains! For the Lord comforts His people and will have compassion on His afflicted ones.
Isaiah 49:13

You are my life, Lord. I can do nothing apart from You. Continue to comfort me. Help me to grieve well. Use my grief for Your plans and purposes.

134

*Certain things have become special to me. Photos.
Objects. Places. Things that remind me of my child.*

*Some of these things were special before, but now they've taken
on a whole new significance. When I see them, I remember. And
when I remember, I feel the anguish, the grief, and the gratitude.*

*My child isn't with me here anymore, but I'm thankful
for them. They were, and are, a gift to me. God personally
created my child. He made all this possible.*

*At first, these reminders brought pain to my heart.
Now, they also bring a new kind of joy. It feels
different. Memories are tinged with grief and sadness,
but also laced with thankfulness and gratitude.*

*I'm so glad my child was in my life, and I in
theirs. I'm hurting, but I'm also blessed.*

After a child dies, the loss takes over our hearts for a while. All we can feel is the grief and the pain. We're shocked and stunned. Life has changed. The world has changed. Our world feels empty now.

As we openly express our hearts to God and share with Him what's happening inside us, we begin to sense His presence with us. We experience His love amid the pain, sadness, anger, and confusion. Over time, He heals our wounded hearts.

This doesn't mean we stop grieving or missing our child. We may always grieve on some level. But the grief is changing. As we allow God to renew our minds while we're hurting, we begin to see things with more perspective. Gratitude for our child and all we experienced with them grows and begins to exert its influence in our hearts.

We find memorials around us—things that remind us of our child and evoke fond memories. These pictures, objects, or places become even more special to us. We remember. We thank God for our children. We thank God for Himself, His love, and His salvation.

"The Lord is my strength and my defense; He has become my salvation. He is my God, and I will praise Him, my father's God, and I will exalt Him."
Exodus 15:2

You have blessed me, Lord. I'm grateful for those You have placed in my life. I will praise You, for You created them and brought our paths together. I will exalt You.

135

*At first, memories of my child brought only pain and
sadness. Now they also bring gratitude and smiles.*

*I don't know when this change took place.
It happened over time, bit by bit.*

*I didn't realize it at first. Then one day I felt different. My smile
had returned. I realized I felt some joy somewhere deep inside.*

*I'm not saying that I'm all better. I've learned enough
to never say that I'm done grieving. I'll always miss
my child. I love them. My grief will continue.*

*But that grief is changing. The color is seeping
back into life, little by little, day by day.*

*At first, I felt guilty feeling anything good. Now I realize that joy
is a gift, and I honor my child when I allow myself to feel it.*

*Like grief, joy can be a way I remember them. They brought much
joy to me, so when I think of them, feeling joyful is natural.*

*It's a mixed bag—a mysterious combo
of grief and gladness.*

Grief and life are certainly a mixed bag. So much variety. So many unexpected twists and turns. So many good things combined with so much tragedy. The ups and downs are extraordinary, and many of them can leave us breathless.

You're describing a healthy grief process. We feel the terrible loss of our child. Sadness, anger, confusion, frustration, and emotional pain invade. Our emotions are all over the place. It takes a toll on us mentally, physically, and spiritually. Our child is no longer here, and the change is stunning and shocking.

Our hearts need time to adjust. We grieve. We long for our child. We hunger for their presence and their voice. We yearn to touch and hold them. We miss them and everything about them. The loss permeates all of life.

Then one day a shift occurs. It's been happening over time, but we haven't noticed. We feel different. Our grief has changed. Our new terrain is growing more familiar somehow. God is healing us.

And He will continue to heal you. He is faithful. He is committed to you. He bathes your wounds in His love.

They will enter Zion with singing;
everlasting joy will crown their heads.
Gladness and joy will overtake them, and
sorrow and sighing will flee away.
Isaiah 35:10

You can turn disaster into blessing. Thank you for bringing gladness and joy back into my life and heart. You are my Healer. I praise You.

136

Just when I think I'm healing, I have another grief burst.

Yesterday's burst was a big one. It came out of nowhere. I couldn't even identify a trigger. I felt terribly sad and distraught. Emotion welled up and spilled out of me.

Afterwards, I felt better, but also embarrassed. I felt like I had done something wrong or gone backwards somehow. I felt like a failure.

I thought, "Great. I can't even do grief right. Where did I go wrong? What is this?"

I'm trying to accept myself in this.

I know I need to be patient with myself, but this feels like such a setback.

I miss my child terribly. I would give almost anything for one more hug.

Grief has no timetable. Grief bursts can come anytime, anywhere, with any intensity, at any stage of our grief process.

When can we honestly say our grief process is done? We know intellectually that we'll always grieve on some level because we'll always miss our children. We're surrounded by reminders, so feeling sadness again isn't surprising.

Yet our hearts want to be past the pain of this terrible loss.

Deep down, we want to honor our children and the Lord with joy and gratitude. We want to live well and allow God to live through us to make a difference in the world around us. Sometimes grief bursts can seem like an enemy trying to scuttle our growth and progress.

Grief bursts are actually more like a broken bone. If we break our leg, we're not surprised at soreness with sudden weather shifts or more exertion than usual. Our leg healed, but it is not the same.

Our hearts are healing, but they are not the same. Grief bursts will come. Ride them out. Feel the grief. Be present as much as possible in the moment.

The Lord is with you in that moment—in every moment. His arms are around you as the grief bursts comes. Rest in Him.

My eyes are ever on the Lord, for only He
will release my feet from the snare.
Psalm 25:15

Lord, I give my emotions and all future grief bursts to You.
Encourage me and remind me that these times are part of your
healing process.
My eyes are on You.

137

I'm hard on myself. I expect ridiculous things of my body, mind, and heart. I guess I think I'm superhuman.

I feel sad, and I judge myself. I talk to myself and try to move out of the sadness into something more pleasant.

I pray. I repeat Scriptures that come to mind. I distract myself.

It's like I've spilled a drink. I'm embarrassed and irritated with myself.

I sigh and rush around trying to wipe it up so there's no trace of the spill remaining. I want my life neat, clean, and mistake free.

How unrealistic is that?

Every time I think I'm doing better, something happens. I feel derailed. I'm disappointed with myself and frustrated with circumstances.

The loss of my child has changed everything. I will never be the same.

Most of us tend to be hard on ourselves in some way. We want to feel competent and somewhat in control of our thoughts, feelings, and behavior.

As grief goes on, we get used to some things, but get irritated with others. After feeling out of control about everything, we're hungry to have some ability to manage what happens in us and around us.

We have ideas in our head about how grief should go. When it doesn't pan out that way, we look in the mirror. We judge ourselves. We're blowing it somehow.

Of course, we know our expectations are unrealistic. Many times, we live according to what we want to be true rather than what really is. We want to be past the unpleasantness of grief.

We live from our hearts. Our child is gone, and our hearts have been badly wounded. These wounds get bumped frequently in daily life, and we feel pain all over again. Nothing is wrong. This is natural and healthy.

God heals our wounds, but His healing process isn't about taking our wounds away. He uses our losses (yes, even this loss) to grow and mature us—to deepen our love for Him and trust in Him.

He never wastes pain. He uses your grief for your good.

The Lord upholds all who fall and lifts up all who are bowed down.
Psalm 145:14

No matter how I feel or what happens, You are with me. You are in me, and I am in You. Heal my heart. Use my wounds for good. Deepen my love for You.

138

I thank God for the people in my life who know grief, especially other grieving parents. They make such a difference.

They care. They listen. They don't judge. They support. They get it.

I'm learning to listen and serve by watching and interacting with them. Just being in their presence brings me a great sense of safety.

Somehow, I know everything is going to be okay, even if it doesn't feel that way.

Other bereaved parents have been gifts from God to me. I want to be a gift to others too. I pray for the patience and love to see people and to listen.

I knew listening was important. Now I know it's one of life's most important skills.

Listening is a huge part of love.

Jesus loved us by entering our worlds and walking with us in our mess. He loved us by giving Himself for us. When we put aside our agendas, see others, and take time to enter their world, amazing things can happen. This is love in action.

Spending time with loving, caring, and inspiring people has a great impact. Our hearts naturally respond. We're created to love God and love people. When we're with others who are doing that, our hearts come alive in new ways.

God puts safe people and other grieving moms and dads in our lives. Jesus gave His life for us so that He could give His life to us and live His life through us. These safe people are allowing that to happen. They are reflections of Jesus to those around them. When this happens, everybody wins.

Even amid the painful loss of a child, God is healing you. He lives in you and wants to live through you to comfort and love others. What an honor it is to be a part of what He is doing. If we're willing, our own suffering can open us up to be used by God in new and even deeper ways.

***There is surely a future hope for you,
and your hope will not be cut off.
Proverbs 23:18***

Thank you for using people to remind me of Your goodness and faithfulness. You have a plan for me. You are my hope. Let me be a hope-bringer to others.

139

The death of my child has caused me to look back and evaluate everything.

I've been blessed. I've blown it many times. My life is an interesting mix of ups and downs.

I guess most people could say that. If I compare, I can always find someone with a better life. I can also find someone who has had it much worse.

What do I know? I'm not on the inside of their lives or hearts. I only know my own.

I find myself thinking about forgiveness a lot. I've forgiven others. Yet old stuff pops up now more than ever. Do I forgive again?

Sometimes I find myself wondering if I need to forgive God. I've held Him responsible for things along the way, without knowing it at the time. I believe I allowed some wounds to distance me from Him.

Is it weird or wrong to forgive God?

Perhaps I need to forgive myself for blaming Him. That sounds more real and true.

In any case, my heart is in forgiveness mode at present, and I want to cover as much ground as possible.

The death of a child can bring clarity and depth to many things, including the importance of forgiveness. Forgiveness is one of life's greatest and most practical skills. It's one of the basic ways we can care for and guard our own hearts.

We forgive as often as necessary. We forgive any time a past wound or offense comes up. We release the offense and the person again. Often the hardest thing is releasing ourselves by accepting God's forgiveness. Most of us carry more against ourselves than we do against anyone else. When you forgive, don't forget about releasing yourself from past errors too.

Of course, God doesn't need our forgiveness. He's perfect and never does anything that is not loving. But we don't always see it this way. We often see Him as responsible for pain—either causing or allowing it—and subconsciously we can begin to distance ourselves from Him. We trust Him, but wall off parts of our hearts at the same time.

God doesn't need us to release Him from blame, but perhaps our own hearts do. Many of us need to release our heavenly Father from blame in order to clear out some of what holds us back from intimacy with Him. Blame always hinders trust.

How do we do this? Ironically, we accept God's forgiveness for blaming Him in the first place. We ask for a mind-shift. We yield to His wisdom and love.

Choose to live in forgiveness. This honors your child and the Lord who created them.

Then Peter came to Jesus and asked, "Lord, how many times shall I forgive my brother or sister who sins against me? Up to seven times?" Jesus answered, "I tell you, not seven times, but seventy times seven times."
Matthew 18:21-22

Broken Walk

Lord, I release all offenses and wrongs done to me by others. I forgive. Help me to forgive frequently and quickly in the future. You live in me. You are an expert at this.

140

I'm still thinking about forgiveness today. In fact, this morning I wrote an "offense" list.

I went back and thought about what has happened in my life. Some things I felt peaceful about, like I had already dealt with those situations. Other events and names triggered emotions that were unpleasant.

I thought about those people and forgave them— again. I even forgave my child for leaving, as strange as that might sound. I forgave them for all I've missed already and all I'm going to miss in the future because they're not here.

I forgave and released all those who disappeared during my grief process—including those who were critical, judgmental, and even mean.

And I released God from blame—for my loved one's death, for the wounds in my life, for other people's behavior, and for bad things that have happened along the way. I asked and received His forgiveness for blaming Him in the first place.

He has done nothing but love me. I was in the wrong.

It felt good. I cleaned my spiritual house. My heart feels lighter. I needed that.

We carry much that we don't have to. Most of us are burdened by weights from the past that we've gotten so used to carrying that we don't notice them anymore. They're still there, weighing us down more than we realize.

Forgiveness is always a good, godly, and holy thing. God is an expert at it. He lives in you. When you forgive, He is working in and through you.

At some point it dawns on us that we're the ones that benefit from forgiving others. We're actually releasing ourselves. Forgiveness isn't saying it didn't matter, but that it mattered deeply—so deeply that we don't want it to scuttle our lives and relationships. When we forgive others, we set our own hearts free.

When our hearts are free, our ability to trust goes up. We have more energy to love. When we forgive, Christ is at work in us in ways we're not aware of—blessing us and all those around us.

We forgive because we begin to realize how much we've been forgiven. Jesus paid the total and complete penalty for our sins. He died in our place on the cross. Once we embrace Him, we are forgiven.

Many times we don't receive that forgiveness. We want to punish ourselves somehow for what we've done or haven't done. We choose to live with these burdens rather than walking in the freedom Christ won for us.

Even amid this heavy grief, we can live in freedom and forgiveness. Jesus is with us—leading us through this deep valley.

---

*Bear with each other and forgive one
another if any of you has a grievance against
someone. Forgive as the Lord forgave you.*
Colossians 3:13

Thank you, Lord, for Your forgiveness. Thank you that You live in me. Work in me to practice forgiveness. Life is heavy, and I want to travel as light as possible.

141

I have so many memories. As I look back, the guilt and regret surfaces—again. I tend to ruminate on that. I can venture into dark places quickly. I'm naturally hard on myself, even about the past.

I hold myself hostage. I know this holds me back. I know this doesn't benefit me or anyone else. Guilt doesn't help me grieve, and it certainly doesn't help my relationship with God.

Yet, I seem to give in to it quickly.

Do I want to punish myself somehow?

When I think of the death of my child, the what-if's come barreling into my mind and heart. I've been over this ground dozens of times. Will I ever be done with guilt?

Ironic that this comes up today after we talked about forgiveness and freedom yesterday.

Guilt is not my friend. I must guard my heart. Sometimes I seem especially vulnerable to guilt's voice.

Guilt can be nasty. It is persistent, persuasive, and relentless. It keeps coming, knocking, and intruding. Guilt can exert powerful influence in our minds and hearts.

Try not to focus on the guilt. Focus gives guilt exactly what it wants—your attention and energy. It wants you all to itself. Guilt is an expert at distraction and discouragement.

Shift your heart from guilt to God's forgiveness. What Christ did for you on the cross was completely effective. All your sin has been paid for and your guilt wiped out. The ledger is clean. There is now no condemnation for you.

Let that sink in. No condemnation. Christ took it all. He has granted you His freedom. You are a new creation now.

Keep releasing the past. Ask God to remind you that you are forgiven and free.

---

*For as high as the heavens are above the earth,
so great is His love for those who fear Him;
as far as the east is from the west, so far has
He removed our transgressions from us.*
Psalm 103:11-12

Lord, let me experience and live the freedom that I have in You. Reassure me of Your love and forgiveness. Empower me to release all that is not helpful in following You.

142

I want to put my grief to work. I want to use it to honor my child. I want all the pain, confusion, and frustration to count.

I want to be a better listener. I want to look into others' eyes and hear more of their hearts. I want God to use me to bring comfort and hope.

I've been comforted in all this—even when the grief was intense. I couldn't see it then, but I can now. God's fingerprints are everywhere. He is loving me, protecting me, guiding me.

I'm still grieving, but I want to give back. I've been thinking about serving somehow in my support group.

Perhaps that's a start.

When we choose to use our grief for fuel, everyone benefits. Our own hearts take a leap of healing. We get out of our own heads and connect with others. We exercise our wounded hearts.

God comforts us in all our troubles, including the terrible loss of a child. There may be times when we don't feel this, but that doesn't change the fact that He is with us, loving us and guiding us.

We can't give away what we don't have, but once we receive God's love and comfort amid pain and loss, it begins to grow in us and eventually spills out of us to those around us. When we serve, we heal a little more.

So much of life is about overcoming. Jesus has overcome the world, and He lives in you. He invites you to be a conduit of His life and love to a hurting world.

Wounded hearts can grow either bitter or compassionate. God uses compassionate, humble hearts to change the world, one soul at a time.

This is to my Father's glory, that you bear much fruit, showing yourselves to be my disciples.
John 15:8

> *Produce Your fruit in me, Lord. Work through me. Love others through me, even while I'm hurting. Use me to bring hope and healing.*

143

I realized something this morning.

The Lord was with my child when they died. He was there. He was with them in the moment. I believe He was loving them in ways that I cannot know.

I don't pretend to understand this. I believe that God is everywhere and that He is loving. He was there. He was somehow expressing His love.

They say we all die alone. I guess that's true in a sense.

But in another way, we're never alone. I choose to believe that the Lord, who loves us, is especially close when death approaches.

My mind doesn't get it, but my heart somehow does.

The Lord is my comfort. He is love.

God works in ways that we do not see, and many times cannot understand. He has perspective that we do not. He knows all things. He is perfect in His wisdom and His love.

Yes, He was with your child in that moment, just as He is here, now. In certain traumatic or even evil situations, this is hard to imagine. I too think that God is especially close in times of pain, danger, and death.

It is easy to forget that He has been through this Himself. There are many traumatic deaths, but none can top what Jesus went through. False accusations, hatred, abuse, betrayal, rejection, beating, and torture, all leading up to a slow and painful death while hanging near naked and exposed for all to see.

He knows. No matter what the situation, He gets it. Yes, He was with your child. He is with us. He is our ultimate friend and confidant.

Even when we don't understand, we can trust. This is part of what it means to walk in faith.

But He was pierced for our transgressions,
He was crushed for our iniquities; the
punishment that brought us peace was on
Him, and by His wounds we are healed.
Isaiah 53:5

You are my constant companion, Lord. You are faithful, even when I am not. I want intimate fellowship with You. You are with me. You are in me. I love You.

144

I think I have been chasing perfection all my life.

I want life to be smooth, beautiful, and delightful. I want my work to be productive and yield good, beneficial results.

I want to live without aging. I want everything to be good all the time.

Sounds ridiculous, but deep down that must be what I want. When it's not that way, I get irritated and upset. No wonder I've struggled with losing my child.

On the one hand, I've never wanted to settle for mediocre or anything less than good.

On the other hand, I seem to have trouble accepting and dealing with things as they are. I'm always trying to change whatever I don't like.

Perhaps I need to accept what I cannot change and focus on loving those around me.

I want to trust the Lord, but sometimes I'm not sure what that looks like.

Most of us try to control situations and people to get what we think we need or what we want. We come out of the womb trying to make life work for us. We often do this without God—or at best with God on the periphery.

We think of this as our life. We ask God to bless us and our plans. We feel betrayed by Him when trouble, pain, or loss invades. We seek comfort. We like smooth and easy.

God invites us to something better. He invites us to experience Him and trust Him amid all the pain and frustration of life. We're continually confronted by the reality that, while we might have influence, we control next to nothing, and anything can happen at any time to anyone.

This is not our life. Life is a gift from Him. It's not about us or our comfort. It's about Him and His plan for crushing evil and being with us forever.

There are many things along the way that we will not understand. Jesus disciples "did not understand" what He was saying and doing on multiple occasions. Though we do not understand, we can choose to trust.

He is life. Life is about Him. He lives in you. You are living His life today. This is His story, and you are a part of it.

***For in Christ all the fullness of the Deity
lives in bodily form, and in Christ you
have been brought to fullness.
Colossians 2:9-10***

*I have You, Lord. Therefore, I have everything.
This is Your story. Thank you for including me.
I want to know You better. You are life.*

145

Perhaps in my pursuit of my own little Garden of Eden, I'm actually longing for heaven. Is that possible?

Now that I've lost my child, I look around me and ask the question, "Is this all there is?"

Loss will do that to a person. I'm thinking about things more deeply now.

This is not all there is. It can't be. God says it isn't. There is so much more.

There is a spiritual reality all around me that I can't see. Things are not simply as they appear.

I wonder what heaven is like. I know it's good. Better than good.

Perhaps heaven is here, all around me, in some way. I don't know. My eyesight is so limited.

We all long for heaven in many ways. We yearn to be loved and accepted as we are. We long to be fully ourselves. We hunger to be free from things that harm, hinder, and bind us.

Most of all, deep down, we're designed to be with the One who thought of us, wanted us, and created us. Only He truly knows who we are.

We thirst for heaven because we long for God Himself. Our hearts stretch to know Him, be with Him, and experience Him without hindrance. We were created to live forever with Him in His immediate presence.

We journey through a foreign wasteland, heading home. Our hearts never feel fully at home here. Tragic and terrible things happen that remind us that this present reality is temporary. We instinctively know there's something more, something greater and better.

We experience His love now. He walks with us here. He gives us glimpses of what's to come. Over time, He can set our minds more on eternal things, giving us perspective for life here and making contentment possible no matter what the circumstances.

He made us for Himself. Nothing less will satisfy our hearts.

For our light and momentary troubles are achieving for us an eternal glory that far outweighs them all. So we fix our eyes not on what is seen, but on what is unseen, since what is seen is temporary, but what is unseen is eternal.
2 Corinthians 4:17-18

Lord, You made me for Yourself. I belong to You. Only You can satisfy my longings. I lean into You. I worship You. I delight in You.

146

*I have many questions. I'm assuming all of them will
be answered one day, but probably not in this life.*

*"Why?" is still the most pressing question. I wonder this about
a lot of things. Then again, there seems to be a part of me that
doesn't have to understand. Perhaps this is the best part of my
heart. I'm learning to be peaceful and to take things as they come.*

*I look back at all the losses. This death of my child has
unearthed all the previous losses and given them life again.*

*Life is hard. Painful. Full of joy at times, yes, but
also permeated with unwanted surprises.*

*Perhaps when I see the Lord, all my questions will evaporate.
Maybe I'll instantly know all the answers I need. I'm certain
that I'll be thrilled, peaceful, and content all at the same time.*

My angst will not enter heaven with me.

*That will be nice. No angst. No under-the
surface grumblings and frustrations.*

Heaven will be far beyond our best expectations. We will finally be exactly who we were designed to be, and the same will be true for everyone around us there.

I have a feeling that when we arrive in heaven our hearts will shout, "Yes! This is what I've dreamed about and longed for all my life and never knew it!" As you said, perhaps all our questions will be answered, or maybe they will simply evaporate because they don't matter anymore.

It will be a wonderful and grand reunion with all those we know and love, who know and love the Lord. I can't imagine the freedom and the unbridled joy and delight. No more sin. No more wondering. No more anxiety or fear.

He is preparing a place for us. He knows us. Only He knows who we truly are. His love is perfect. He will complete the work He started in us. He is faithful. We have much to look forward to.

Set your minds on things above, not on earthly things. For you died, and your life is now hidden with Christ in God. When Christ, who is your life, appears, then you also will appear with him in glory.
Colossians 3:2-4

Lord, give me heavenly eyes. Set my mind on You. Enable me to see reality as it is. Help me to trust You. I release all my questions to You.

147

I don't sit still very well. Most of my prayers are what I call "flare prayers." I fire them spontaneously, here and there, during the day.

I don't rest well either, especially since the loss of my child. However, it's getting a little better over time. I'm finding my emotional footing again—at least somewhat. My heart seems a little calmer and more settled.

I'm not the same, and I never will be. I don't want to be the same. I want to heal and grow.

I see things more clearly now. I control so little. Prayer is the most powerful thing I can do—for myself and for others.

I want to offer more than flare prayers. I am making a list. There is so much to pray for.

I want to take time each day to pray. I want to pray throughout the day. I want prayer to be my lifestyle.

I want to pray for people when I see them, while I'm talking to them, and anytime I think about them.

God is certainly using others' prayers in my life. I'm grateful.

God is remarkably generous. He invited us to participate in what He is doing, even as we're missing our child and grieving. Prayer is a huge part of that.

Prayer isn't so much about asking for things, but rather it's a conversation with the Almighty One. We're sharing our hearts with Him.

We're intentionally thinking out loud in His presence. We're being open, real, and authentic with Him. He invites us to ask, seek, and knock. We're healthiest when we live openly with Him and pray about everything. Prayer isn't about results, but rather about companionship.

As we pray, we trust. We share our hearts with Him. We ask. We leave things in His hands. We watch to see what He will do. He is always at work, and He is certainly at work in and through our prayers.

"Pray continuously," Paul said. Prayer and trusting our Father is not a task, but a lifestyle—a continual condition of our hearts.

Devote yourselves to prayer, being watchful and thankful.
Colossians 4:2

Remind me, Lord, that prayer is conversation with You.
Give me the power to be real and share my heart with You.
Speak to me. Deepen and enrich my walk with You.

148

I often wonder what to pray for. Do others wonder about this?

I end up praying for the results I want—in my own life or someone else's—and then saying something like, "Your will be done, Lord." I pray my desires, but I'm not sure I pray with much faith.

My child's death has brought me to question this.

It seems there are so many unanswered prayers. I pray, but sometimes I wonder what's the point if God's will is going to be done anyway.

Is there a way to know what God's will is? Then I could pray with confidence and faith.

At least, I think I could.

I wonder what to pray for myself. What is His will for me?

There is much we don't know, but thankfully there are things we can know for certain. These are the things that God has revealed to us in His word about Himself, about us, and about life.

There are things that we know are God's will—all the time, no matter what. That we love Him and express that love with our lives. That we seek Him and trust Him. That we allow Him to live through us to love others. That we immerse ourselves in His Word and allow His thoughts to penetrate and fill our minds and hearts.

These are things we can pray for with confidence and faith for ourselves and every person we meet. We might not know God's specific will about this or that, but we do know He longs for us to experience Him and His love amid all the trouble of this life – even after the loss of a child.

God invites us to set our minds on heavenly things—on spiritual reality—and pray accordingly. As we do this, we see more of the larger picture.

If you remain in me and my words remain in you, ask whatever you wish, and it will be done for you.
John 15:7

I want to know You better, Lord. The better I know You, the clearer I will discern Your will. I give myself again to You. You are my life.

149

Life is about a relationship with God. It must be. Nothing else makes sense. Nothing else satisfies. The loss of my child has made this clear to me.

Yet, I'm amazed how quickly I can wander from this.

I get caught up in my own stuff—the daily routine, responsibilities, and the flurry of interruptions and unexpected obstacles.

God gets shoved to the periphery quickly.

Sometimes I lay my head on the pillow at night and realize I haven't thought of Him all day. Sad. Who knows what opportunities I've missed?

After the loss of my child, I'm on a mission to live life well. I want to make the most of each moment.

God is patient with us. We tend to be impatient with ourselves.

When you get frustrated, consider that as God's invitation to return to what you know to be true. He is real. He is sovereign and works out all things for His glory and our good. He loves you. He is perfect. He is your life. He is your home.

No matter how distracted we get, these things never change, because He never changes. On our worst day, His love for us is still perfect and His commitment to us still total. As we rest in Him and all the certainties that surround Him, our hearts relax more. Instead of holding ourselves hostage with guilt, we sigh, look to the Lord, and ask Him to continue to fill us and live through us.

It's not what happened or what we did or didn't do but what we do next that matters most now. He invites us to be still and know that He is God. He is certain. He is sure.

We are learning and growing, even while enduring this deep, terrible loss of our child. He is patient and completely committed to us.

He will complete what He has begun in us. This is certain because He is certain.

Your kingdom is an everlasting kingdom, and Your dominion endures through all generations. The Lord is trustworthy in all he promises and faithful in all he does.
Psalm 145:13

Lord, You are my rock and my fortress. You are my provision, my strength, and my life. You are faithful. Live through me and accomplish Your will today.

150

I'm asking God to use this pain—the loss of my child—for good somehow. Along with that, I'm asking Him to use all past pain for good too.

I can look back and see Him doing that. I can also see it in this case, but not so clearly yet. I guess I need time and distance to discern more.

He is always doing more than I can see or know.

I choose to believe that He is good, no matter how things appear. I put aside my fickle judgments based on my shortsighted, human view of things.

Amid this pain, I choose to trust and rest in Him.

Use the pain, Lord. Use the losses, the emotions, the confusion, and all the changes.

Heal me. Heal others. Use me.

God is a master at turning tragedy and pain into good. He is the ultimate turnaround artist.

He is always at work, loving us and loving others through us. He is always taking what happens—even terrible tragedy—and turning it around and using it to accomplish His will.

As we've said before, He never wastes pain. He speaks to us in our distress. He heals broken, wounded hearts. He enters our messes with us. He walks with us in our grief and confusion.

He uses wounded, imperfect people who are willing. He uses us even when we're unaware. He is always at work in us—speaking to our hearts, comforting us, and bringing hope. He gives peace, even in the direst circumstances.

Trust is a choice, as you said. We choose to trust now, in this moment, and then in the next moment. We contemplate His limitless love that He continually lavishes on us. We rest.

It is God who arms me with strength and keeps my way secure. He makes my feet like the feet of a deer; He causes me to stand on the heights.
2 Samuel 22:33-34

You know me, Lord. Use me. Use all my weaknesses and failures for good. Turn everything around and use it for Your purposes. Rivet my attention on You.

151

*I accept the truth that God is loving. More than
that, I accept the truth that He loves us.*

He loves me.

*"For God so loved the world..." I used to think He
had to love me because I was part of the package deal.
He had to love everyone, so He loved me too.*

*It's stunning to think that the Creator of the universe— the One
who sustains everything—loves me, individually and personally.*

*He knows me. He knows my heart, my mind. He
thought of me, wanted me, and created me. He
died for me and rose from the dead for me.*

For all of us. For me.

*As I grieve this awful loss, I will remember that God
loves me. He is at work, even through all of this.
He somehow works out all things for my good, even
through the terrible pain of losing my child.*

I will trust Him.

In the book of Ephesians, Paul prays that believers might know the love of Christ that surpasses all knowledge. The word "know" here goes beyond head knowledge to personal experience. Paul prays that we might continually experience the never-ending, measureless, limitless love of Christ.

If we know we're completely and totally loved, it makes a massive difference in our hearts and lives. When we realize that God is not fickle, and that there is nothing we can do to cause Him to love us any more or any less, our lives turn from worry and fear to gratitude and trust. Peace permeates. Joy wells up within.

We are perfectly loved by a perfect God who always loves perfectly. He is love. He is the very definition of goodness, care, compassion, and unconditional commitment. Once we trust in Christ, He lives in us and we in Him. We are now one spirit with Him. Relationship doesn't get any closer than that.

Our experience lags far behind the reality. The pain of this life, including the loss of a child, can dull our perception of God's love and goodness.

The truth is almost too good to believe. But believe it we do. We receive. He is love. He loves us.

But whoever is united with the
Lord is one spirit with Him.
1 Corinthians 6:17

I am in You. You are in me. I am one spirit with You. I am stunned by Your goodness and love. Let me experience more of Your love with each passing day.

152

*I'm hurting, but I refuse to let the pain
win. I want to find ways to serve.*

I'm still vulnerable. I guess I'm always vulnerable.

*God says He shows Himself in and through my weaknesses. If He
uses me when I'm like this, it's certainly not me doing it. It's Him.*

*I choose to believe that as I serve, I will be blessed and continue
to heal. I don't want to serve to get, however, but to give. I
want to be a channel of God's love and compassion to others.*

As I give, I receive. I'm receiving all the time.

*I'm tired. Many times, I'm exhausted. I need balance
and wisdom. I trust that God will give me these.*

I will lean into Him and let Him lead.

God will bring service opportunities to you. In fact, He probably already has. And yes, He uses us greatly in times of personal weakness.

The fact is we're all weak. When we reach out to others in our weakness, they respond. They know we get it. We understand.

Most people are hurting, tired, frustrated, worried, and afraid. Few will admit this, of course. We're good at wearing our masks and playing our roles. Underneath the mask, however, many of us are screaming for healing, hope, peace, and love.

As we receive God's love, it naturally begins to spill out of us and onto those around us. As we trust Him, it opens up pathways for Him to declare His love and care through us. He is the light. He shines through us—his cracked pots.

Broken, but healing. Wounded, yet loving. Scared at times, yet hopeful. Willing to trust and to be used for good, even now, after this devastating loss. That's us.

Therefore, my dear brothers and sisters, stand firm. Let nothing move you. Always give yourselves fully to the work of the Lord, because you know that your labor in the Lord is not in vain.
1 Corinthians 15:58

Knowing You, Lord, is my goal and my desire. This is the priority of my life. You are my life. Light of the world, shine through me.

153

I'm trying to trust, but things seem dark some days.

There are times when my emotions get the better of me. Sadness takes over. Questions swirl in my mind. A tinge of hopelessness comes out of nowhere and colors everything.

I miss my child.

I try to ignore all this and chase it away somehow. I feel like I'm being invaded, and I fight against it. I end up stuffing the sadness to keep my mask in place.

It feels like I'm hiding. I want to be over this somehow. I want to feel better. I'm tired of sadness.

Why does life have to be so heavy and lonely?

Am I doing something wrong? Have I missed something? Shouldn't I be better by now?

Then there's a part of me that doesn't want to get better. I want to be sad because that means I remember.

Breathe. Slow down and breathe. We're certainly in a battle.

Grief, however, is not something to be fought. It is not the enemy. Grief is the natural and healthy response to a loss, especially the loss of a child.

If we ignore and stuff our emotions, we give them more power over us. We store them away to work secretly inside us and spread their influence in less-than-obvious ways.

The more we stuff our feelings, the more they will leak out, often in unhealthy ways. Grief will be expressed, one way or another. It's better to acknowledge the emotions when they hit. Go ahead and feel them, as much as you can. Process them by talking, writing, or drawing. Feel them through, so that your body and mind can release them.

God isn't threatened by our emotions. He isn't shocked by our feelings. He doesn't take a step back, roll His eyes, and say, "Now, now. Get that under control."

Instead, He simply invites us to be real with Him and share what's happening inside us. The more we do this, the safer we feel. The safer we feel, the more we tend to trust.

The more we trust, the more peace we have. The more peace we have, the more we heal and grow.

You, Lord, are my lamp; the Lord turns my darkness into light.
2 Samuel 22:29

Enable me to rest in You, Lord. You accept me as I am. You love me. You are my safety and security. You are my peace.

154

*I don't know how many times I have to experience
it to get it. Grief is not a straight road.*

*It's not a clear, smooth path. It's a meandering,
obstacle-ridden, can-hardly-see-in-front-of-you
path through a thick forest laden with fog.*

*As I heal, I'm still surprised by emotion at times. Grief
sneaks up on me. Healing is an up-and-down process.
Life isn't smooth. I keep telling myself this.*

*I'm to the point where I don't like surprises much.
Lately, most of the big surprises haven't been
good. I want stability and predictability.*

*Yet, as I write that, I know I have stability in the
Lord. He is sure and certain. I must rest in Him.*

*The loss of my child has been difficult beyond description. It still
is. I've had plenty of loss in the past, so you would think I would
know all this by now. Sometimes, I feel like I know nothing.*

I guess I'm still learning. Maybe I'm just human.

*I'm healing and growing. God is good. He
loves me. He carries me through.*

We try to prepare ourselves for what's coming, even though we don't know what that is. After the traumatic loss of a child, we don't want to be surprised again by more loss and pain. Even subconsciously, we begin constructing life to protect ourselves and those we love.

We worry. We fret. Our minds spin. We live on the edge of our seats, waiting for the next unwanted hit.

On top of this, life bumps our wounds. Grief from past losses can suddenly surface again with shocking intensity. This is natural, common, and healthy. Bumped wounds should hurt.

As we walk with God through this, He teaches us. He gives us perspective, one little bit at a time. We get it intellectually, but it takes time and experience for it to trickle down into our hearts. Life is not about getting it right or never failing again. Life is about walking with God amid all the unpredictability.

He is certain. He knows. He is ordering all things for your good. He is working with all that happens and using it for His purposes. He lives in us. We live in Him. Conscious companionship with Him is what our hearts long for.

Therefore, if anyone is in Christ, the new creation has come: The old has gone, the new is here!
2 Corinthians 5:17

I am a new creation. You have done this, Lord. Christ now lives in me. Companionship with You is my heart's true desire. Make me more aware of You today.

155

My perspective is changing. I can feel it. The grief is changing too. I don't know how to describe it. It's just different.

I feel different. I still miss my child desperately. I always will.

I still get triggered by this or that. Sometimes the grief is so intense I wonder if I can stand it. Yet things have settled in somehow. The loss has become part of me.

My child is a part of me.

My heart is still shattered. At first, all I could feel was the pain. I didn't know that God was there pouring His light into me. Cracks in the heart can go both ways. God enables grief to pour out while He pours Himself in.

I would have said before this loss that God was my constant companion, but now I have experienced His companionship in a new and deeper way. The way of pain and grief can also be the path of growth and healing.

God says these kinds of things over and over in His word. Life's bumps and bruises continually challenge my heart. Am I going to live based on circumstances, or what God has said?

Things are not what they appear. There's always more going on than meets the eye. There are spiritual realities all around us that we cannot see. God is continually at work in ways we are unaware of.

Pain, suffering, tragedy, and death are part of this world. Our hearts rail against this, for we are eternal beings created for relationship. We are spiritual beings, with souls, housed in bodies. This world is not our home. Things happen here that are wrong, unthinkable, and even evil.

Walking with God is the only solution. This is what we were created for—to know and love Him first. When this priority is neglected, our hearts waver, our clarity wanes, and life becomes foggy.

Loss, grief, and suffering can be a pathway to peace. God uses these things to prepare us for our ultimate home and for powerful, meaningful service here. Jesus knows all about suffering, pain, and grief. He walks with us in ours. Our experience of Him grows and deepens.

__Do not let your hearts be troubled. You believe in God; believe also in me. My Father's house has many rooms; if that were not so, would I have told you that I am going there to prepare a place for you? And if I go and prepare a place for you, I will come back and take you to be with me that you also may be where I am.__
__John 14:1-3__

Lord, You live in me. I live in You. I am one spirit with You.
You are preparing a place for me. I am with You now.
I will be with You forever.
I live in certainty. You are my life.

156

I've wondered about a lot through this excruciating loss. Now, I mostly wonder about two things: What is heaven like, and what will life be like for me here now?

There's no way I can know fully about either, but I can know a little. I can know what God has said and what He has revealed. When I don't know something, I'll go to what I do know.

I know that heaven will be better than I can imagine. I know that I will be with God face to face, without any hindrances. I know that when I get there, everything will make sense—or perhaps that won't even matter anymore.

I know life is about walking with God, learning from Him, experiencing Him, and serving Him. Life is about Him. My little story is a part of His grand story. He is my life.

Even while I'm grieving the terrible loss of my child, life is about choosing to trust God, moment by moment. I look forward to the grand reunion to come.

God has shared about heaven with us more than we realize. He is preparing a place for us and is preparing us for that place. One day, there will be no more death, crying, mourning, or pain. All will be life, love, peace, and joy.

We will finally be as we should be. We will be who we really are. No more relational strain or conflict. All regrets of this life will be swallowed up by grace, forgiveness, and goodness. The reunions that take place will be stunning. We will be home.

Yes, this life—all life—is about God. He gave His life for us, so that He could give His life to us, so that He could live His life in and through us. It's all about Him, and He has included us. His goodness and love know no bounds.

This life is anything but smooth and comfortable. Our losses can be unbelievably painful. Our grief can be overwhelming and unpredictable. Yet, God is certain. He never changes. He is victorious over evil, disaster, and death.

We are in Christ. He is victorious. Therefore, we are also victorious. Because He has overcome the world, we too are overcomers. When we live out this truth, we experience Him—His love, peace and joy, even while enduring this deep grief.

He is at the center of all things. When we allow Him to rule our hearts, we heal and grow.

And I heard a loud voice from the throne saying, "Look! God's dwelling place is now among the people, and He will dwell with them. They will be His people, and God Himself will be with them and be their God. He will wipe every tear from their eyes. There will be no more death or mourning or crying or pain, for the old order of things has passed away."
Revelation 21:3-4

Lord, give me eternal perspective. Set my mind on heaven. Produce Your work in and through me. Let me experience You continually.

157

I'm living on borrowed time. We all are. I look back and am stunned at the time and energy I've wasted on things that didn't matter.

My actions betrayed me. My heart was set on earthly things—the here and now and what was happening to me and around me. No wonder I plotted and planned, rushed and strove. No wonder I was derailed by each hardship, obstacle, or death.

I see more clearly now, and I'm grateful. I'm slowly accepting the loss of my child, but I know I'll never get over it.

You never get over a person, especially a child. With God's help, I'll get through pain and learn to love more deeply because of it.

I realize now that everything counts. Everything matters. I want to count. I want the rest of my days to be used for great good.

May your will be done, Lord, in my life as it is in heaven. You are life. You are my life. I love you.

The stakes are high. Hearts everywhere are hurting and grieving. Many have lost hope. Some had little hope to begin with. To many, life is dark.

We know the Light. Jesus said, "I am the light of the world." He also told us, "You are the light of the world." He is the Light, and He lives in us. We are light. Every day, we have opportunities to shine.

We don't shine by trying. We're brightest when we trust. He shines, all the time, everywhere. He shines in us.

As we walk with Him, connected with Him and centered on Him, His light naturally shines through us. There's a fine line between trying to serve Him in our own strength and simply trusting Him to work in and through us for His good pleasure. The first option is a spiritual treadmill of effort. The second is the way of surrendered peace where we are tuned to His voice.

We make the most of the time we've been given by walking with Him, learning from Him, and trusting Him. When we do this, He lives through us and produces His fruit.

He can bring much fruit through terrible disaster. He wastes nothing, especially the loss of a child. Jesus lives in us. He knows and feels our grief. He is with us, in us, and we are in Him.

For everyone born of God overcomes the world. This is the victory that has overcome the world, even our faith. Who is it that overcomes the world? Only the one who believes that Jesus is the Son of God.
1 John 5:4-5

Lord, You have overcome the world. You live in me. You have made me an overcomer. Fill me and live through me. Help me to trust You more.

158

Grief is not for sissies. Neither is life. This is tough stuff. I'm small and limited. I can't do it, but the Lord can. The Lord is up to the challenge. Nothing is impossible for Him.

I can do it in and through Him. I can do all things through Christ, who is my strength.

I miss my child. I'm going to continue to be honest about my pain and grief. I'm going to look for other grieving hearts out there. We need each other. We need compassion, understanding, and acceptance.

I don't know what life will be like now, but I guess I don't need to know. God knows. He is my shepherd, and He is leading. I can trust Him.

Sometimes I don't know exactly what trusting Him means. He will reveal it to me at the right time.

Life is a step-by-step adventure with Him.

When we feel seen, heard, and accepted, we feel a little safer. When we have a sense of safety, our hearts open to healing and growth. Our walls come down—not just with safe people, but with God, as well.

You are the aroma of Christ. He lives in you and wants to live through you. As you trust Him, you allow Him to do that.

He reveals Himself. He touches and loves others through you, even as you continue to endure the loss of your child.

In the process, you heal and grow as well. Everyone wins.

Christ Himself lives in you. He is an expert at grief, healing, and growth. He is perfectly compassionate, always sees things accurately, and always loves. He loves you, and nothing and no one can ever separate you from Him or His perfect love for you.

Even though your child is no longer here, you are loved, valuable, and safe. God is in you and surrounds you. You are in Him. All is well with your soul.

He who was seated on the throne said, "I am making everything new!" Then He said, "Write this down, for these words are trustworthy and true." He said to me: "It is done. I am the Alpha and the Omega, the Beginning and the End. To the thirsty I will give water without cost from the spring of the water of life.
Revelation 21:5-6

Lord, I rest in You. Nurture me. Heal me. Guide me. Fill me. Use me.
Live through me. I am Yours.

Concluding Thoughts

Life is full of loss. The death of a child is uniquely painful and devastating.

God our Father, as the ultimate parent, understands this.

God walks with us through this deep, dark valley.

In our brokenness, He comforts us, speaks to us, and guides us.

He knows what we feel.

He heals us.

He never wastes loss or pain.

He uses all that happens to us as fuel to produce eternal good in our lives and the lives of those around us.

So much of life is about overcoming.

You are an overcomer.

He lives in you. He wants to live through you.

Lean into Him. He is your comfort. He is your life.

Rest. Trust. Walk with Him.

This is His story, and you are a part of it.

Additional Grief Resources

THE COMFORT SERIES

www.garyroe.com/comfort-series

Comfort for Grieving Hearts: Hope and Encouragement in Times of Loss

Comfort for the Grieving Spouse's Heart: Hope and Healing After Losing Your Partner

Comfort for the Grieving Adult Child's Heart: Hope and Healing After Losing Your Parent

Comfort for the Grieving Parent's Heart: Hope and Healing After Losing Your Child

THE GOOD GRIEF SERIES

Aftermath: Picking Up the Pieces After a Suicide

www.garyroe.com/aftermath

Shattered: Surviving the Loss of a Child

www.garyroe.com/shattered

Teen Grief: Caring for the Grieving Teenage Heart

www.garyroe.com/teengrief

Please Be Patient, I'm Grieving: How to Care for and Support the Grieving Heart

www.garyroe.com/please-be-patient

Heartbroken: Healing from the Loss of a Spouse

www.garyroe.com/heartbroken-2

Surviving the Holidays Without You: Navigating Loss During Special Seasons

www.garyroe.com/surviving-the-holidays

THE DIFFERENCE MAKER SERIES

www.garyroe.com/difference-maker

Difference Maker: Overcoming Adversity and Turning Pain into Purpose, Every Day (Adult & Teen Editions)

Living on the Edge: How to Fight and Win the Battle for Your Mind and Heart (Adult & Teen Editions)

Free on Gary's Website

GRIEF: 9 THINGS I WISH I HAD KNOWN

In this deeply personal and practical eBook, Gary shares nine key lessons from his own grief journeys. "This was so helpful! I saw myself on every page," said one reader. "I wish I had read this years ago," said another. Widely popular, this eBook has brought hope and comfort to thousands of grieving hearts.

Available at **www.garyroe.com/free**

THE GOOD GRIEF MINI-COURSE

Full of personal stories, inspirational content, and practical assignments, this 8-session email series is designed to help readers understand grief and deal with its roller-coaster emotions. Thousands have been through this course, which is now being used in support groups as well.

Available at **www.garyroe.com/free**

THE HOLE IN MY HEART:
TACKLING GRIEF'S TOUGH QUESTIONS

This eBook tackles some of grief's big questions: "How did this happen?" "Why?" "Am I crazy?" "Am I normal?" "Will this get any easier?" plus others. Written in the first person, it engages and comforts the heart.

Available at **www.garyroe.com**.

I MISS YOU: A HOLIDAY SURVIVAL KIT

Thousands have downloaded this brief, easy-to-read, and very personal e-book. I Miss You provides some basic, simple tools on how to use holiday and special times to grieve well and love those around you.

Available at **www.garyroe.com/free**

Help us reach other grieving hearts.
Share this link:
https://www.garyroe.com/god-and-grief-series

About the Author

Gary's story began with a childhood of mixed messages and sexual abuse. This was followed by other losses and numerous grief experiences.

Ultimately, a painful past led Gary into a life of helping wounded people heal and grow. A former college minister, missionary in Japan, entrepreneur in Hawaii, pastor, and hospice chaplain, he now serves as a writer, speaker, chaplain, and grief counselor.

In addition to *Broken Walk*, Gary is the author of numerous books, including the award-winning bestsellers *Shattered: Surviving the Loss of a Child*, *Comfort for the Grieving Spouse's Heart*, *Comfort for the Grieving Adult Child's Heart*, and *Aftermath: Picking Up the Pieces After a Suicide*. Gary's books have won four international book awards and have been named finalists seven times. He has been featured on Dr. Laura, Belief Net, the Christian Broadcasting Network, Wellness, Thrive Global, and other major media and has well over 800 grief-related articles in print. Recipient of the Diane Duncam Award for Excellence in Hospice Care, Gary is a popular keynote, conference, and seminar speaker at a wide variety of venues.

Gary loves being a husband and father. He has seven adopted children, including three daughters from Colombia. He enjoys hockey, corny jokes, good puns, and colorful Hawaiian shirts. Gary and his wife Jen and family live in Texas. Visit Gary at **www.garyroe.com**.

Download your exclusive, free, printable PDF:
Scriptures and Prayers from the
God and Grief Series:
www.garyroe.com/grief-prayers

Acknowledgments

Special thanks to my wife Jen for her constant and unwavering support and encouragement. Thank you for engaging with me in giving hope and bringing healing.

Special thanks to Kelli Levey Reynolds and my amazing Advance Reader Team for their keen proofreading eyes and editorial assistance. I appreciate you more than you know.

Thanks to Glendon Haddix of Streetlight Graphics for his artistic skill and expertise in design and formatting. Your artistry continues to bring healing and hope to many.

An Urgent Plea

HELP OTHER GRIEVING HEARTS

Dear Reader,

Others are hurting and grieving today. You can help.

How?

With a simple, heartfelt review.

Could you take a few moments and write a 1-3 sentence review of *Broken Walk* and leave it on the site you purchased the book from?

And if you want to help even more, you could leave the same review on the *Broken Walk* book page on Goodreads.

Your review counts and will help reach others who could benefit from this book.

Thanks for considering this.

I read these reviews as well, and your comments and feedback assist me in producing more quality resources for grieving hearts.

Thank you!
Warmly,
Gary

www.ingramcontent.com/pod-product-compliance
Lightning Source LLC
Chambersburg PA
CBHW030146100526
44592CB00009B/140